Twayne's English Authors Series

Sylvia E. Bowman, *Editor*

INDIANA UNIVERSITY

John Ford

(TEAS) 129

JOHN FORD

By DONALD K. ANDERSON, JR.

University of Missouri

Twayne Publishers, Inc.   ::   New York

Copyright © 1972 by Twayne Publishers, Inc.

All Rights Reserved

Library of Congress Catalog Card Number: 74-180740

PR
2527
.45

MANUFACTURED IN THE UNITED STATES OF AMERICA

66760

FOR
KATHLEEN

Preface

Since 1800, the plays of John Ford have attracted the attention of numerous critics, including such luminaries as Charles Lamb, William Hazlitt, James Russell Lowell, Algernon Swinburne, Hippolyte Taine, and T. S. Eliot. Since 1935 they have been the subject of seven books (the most recent one appearing in 1968). Yet, having for the past twenty years studied both Ford and Fordian scholarship, I have concluded that in three respects the modern view of his work needs clarification: first, the terms most frequently used to describe his plays do not apply to all of them and should, therefore, be used more carefully; second, a preoccupation with two great dramas (*'Tis Pity She's a Whore* and *The Broken Heart*) has resulted in the neglect of two excellent ones (*The Lover's Melancholy* and *Perkin Warbeck*); and third, there has been inadequate recognition of Ford's dramaturgy, his skill in the art of putting together a play. The present book attempts to rectify this picture.

Since the order in which Ford wrote his plays is unknown, to emphasize development or evolution among them seems hazardous. My own sequence, perforce arbitrary, is based upon a combination of facts and judgments. *The Lover's Melancholy*, the first to be discussed, has the earliest known date (it was licensed in 1628); *The Lady's Trial*, the last to be discussed, has the latest date (it was licensed in 1638). Because *The Broken Heart* and *Perkin Warbeck* strike me as being similar to *The Lover's Melancholy*, I group these two former plays with the latter; because *'Tis Pity* and *Love's Sacrifice*, in my opinion, have much in common, I next turn to them; and because *The Fancies* and *The Lady's Trial* impress me the least, I cover both in a single chapter. This order is not crucial, for my principal concern is to analyze each drama in terms of itself as a work of art.

While emphasizing these seven extant plays written solely and unquestionably by Ford (Chapters 4 through 9), I also discuss his nondramatic works (Chapter 2), his collaborations with Thomas Dekker (Chapter 3), and *The Queen* (Chapter 3), of which Ford is the probable author. The Selected Bibliography at the end of the volume includes the more important books and articles about Ford, many of which are mentioned in the text or in Notes and References. The interested reader should consult the secondary sources themselves and, of course, should study Ford's plays.

I wish to express my gratitude to the Folger Shakespeare Library, which awarded me a fellowship for the summer of 1965, and to the University of Missouri, which provided a research grant for the summer of 1966. To Mrs. Norma Davis, a most competent typist; to Mr. Dowling Campbell, a most conscientious graduate assistant; and to my wife, a most valuable champion and critic, I also offer my sincere thanks.

Quotations from most of Ford's works (*The Lover's Melancholy, Love's Sacrifice, The Lady's Trial, The Fancies, The Witch of Edmonton, The Sun's Darling, Fame's Memorial, Honour Triumphant,* and *A Line of Life*) come from the 1895 revision of Gifford's 1827 edition. Those from *The Broken Heart, Perkin Warbeck,* and *'Tis Pity* come from the more recent editions of the Regents Renaissance Drama Series, published by the University of Nebraska Press; those from *The Queen,* from Bang's 1906 edition; and those from *Christ's Bloody Sweat, The Golden Mean,* and *The Spanish Gypsy,* from seventeenth-century editions.

DONALD K. ANDERSON, JR.

University of Missouri

Contents

Preface

Chronology

1. Ford and His Age   13
2. Nondramatic Works   17
3. Collaborations and *The Queen*   33
4. Psychotherapy as Spectacle: *The Lover's Melancholy*   47
5. The Decorum of Dying: *The Broken Heart*   61
6. "Impostor beyond Precedent": *Perkin Warbeck*   77
7. A Sister's Heart: *'Tis Pity She's a Whore*   92
8. Lust and No Lust: *Love's Sacrifice*   107
9. *The Fancies Chaste and Noble* and *The Lady's Trial*   119
10. Ford and the Critics; Conclusion   133

Notes and References   143

Selected Bibliography   149

Index   157

Chronology

1586 John Ford baptised April 17 in Ilsington, Devonshire; second son of Thomas Ford.

1601 Possible short residence at Oxford.

1602 Admitted to the Middle Temple, November 16.

1605 Expelled from the Middle Temple for failure to pay buttery bill.

1606 The poem *Fame's Memorial* and pamphlet *Honour Triumphant* published. Commendatory verses for Barnabe Barnes's *Four Books of Offices* and John Cooper's *Funeral Tears*.

1608 Reinstated at the Middle Temple, June 10.

1610 Bequeathed ten pounds upon his father's death.

1613 The poem *Christ's Bloody Sweat* and pamphlet *The Golden Mean* published.

1616 Bequeathed twenty pounds a year upon the death of his older brother, Henry.

1617 One of forty members of the Middle Temple to be reprimanded for wearing hats instead of lawyers' caps.

1620 The pamphlet *A Line of Life* published.

1621 *The Witch of Edmonton,* written with Dekker and William Rowley, performed at Whitehall.

1623 *The Spanish Gypsy,* first printed in 1653 as by Thomas Middleton and Rowley (but Ford possibly a collaborator or the sole author), licensed. Commendatory verses for John Webster's *The Duchess of Malfi* and Henry Cockeram's *The English Dictionary.*

1624 *The Sun's Darling,* with Dekker, licensed.

1628   *The Lover's Melancholy* licensed; published in 1629. Commendatory verses for James Shirley's *The Wedding* and Philip Massinger's *The Roman Actor*.

1632   Commendatory verses for Richard Brome's *The Northern Lass*.

1633   *The Broken Heart, 'Tis Pity She's a Whore*, and *Love's Sacrifice* published.

1634   *Perkin Warbeck* published.

1636   Commendatory verses for Massinger's *The Great Duke of Florence*.

1638   Commendatory verses for *Jonsonus Virbius*.

1639   *The Lady's Trial*, with dedication by Ford, published. No certain subsequent record of him.

1653   The anonymous *The Queen*, probably by Ford, published. The date of Ford's death is unknown.

CHAPTER 1

Ford and His Age

JOHN FORD, on the basis of his seven (perhaps eight) extant plays, is today considered the outstanding dramatist in the reign of Charles I (1625–49), his reputation surpassing that of his two principal rivals, Philip Massinger and James Shirley. He also ranks high among all English playwrights who, between the accession of Elizabeth in 1558 and the closing of the theaters by the Puritans in 1642, gave to the world that great body of literature now called "Elizabethan drama." The top rung on the ladder belongs to Shakespeare; the second, to Christopher Marlowe and Ben Jonson. On the third, usually with George Chapman, John Webster, Thomas Middleton, and John Fletcher, we find Ford.

Four of Ford's plays are tragedies; the rest, tragicomedies. Two of the former, *'Tis Pity She's a Whore* and *The Broken Heart*, are generally recognized as his best works. The order in which he wrote his plays is not known. The only dates we have for them refer to licensing, printing, or performances; they fall within one decade, 1628–38. Three of the dramas were first printed in the same year, 1633, but they probably were written over a longer period of time; some of the dramas quite possibly were written before 1628.[1] Despite these uncertainties, Ford's literary career can be divided into three chronological periods: 1606 to 1620, for his nondramatic works (two poems and three essays); 1621 to 1625, for his collaborations with other dramatists (chiefly Dekker); and 1625 to 1638, for his unaided plays.

What characterizes Ford's dramatic genius? Many different answers have been given; frequently, however, he has been called decadent, aristocratic, and analytical. Each of these labels is warranted but not without qualification. Although *'Tis Pity She's a Whore,* which presents incest not unfavorably, probably should be called "decadent," most of Ford's other plays, including *The Broken Heart,* should not. Although several dramas are aristocratic in that their leading figures speak and act with regal decorum, an equal number, including *'Tis Pity,* feature middle-class personae who are much less restrained. And, although Ford is in a sense analytical because of his forceful depiction of suffering, he makes relatively little use of the soliloquy; in one play, *Perkin Warbeck,* he gives us no inkling as to the innermost thoughts of his protagonist. Again, the dramatist's undeniable poetic power has frequently been praised for its slow cadences and suppressed emotion—an encomium deserved but incomplete; for it ignores the many other notes, some of them deliberately harsh or loud, in Ford's orchestration.

The aim of this book is not to provide a final formula, an irrefutable common denominator, for the plays of John Ford. Such a quest tends to blur distinctions, to oversimplify. Instead, I hope to contribute some ideas about each of his dramas by examining it individually as a unique creation. At the same time, several generalizations come to mind. One is Ford's abiding interest in and sympathy for love between man and woman, a concern dominating most of his plays and appearing in all of them; this is not the case with Shakespeare, Marlowe, and Jonson. And, with the exception of Act I of *'Tis Pity* and probably Act II of *Love's Sacrifice,* Fordian drama is not erotic; herein it differs from that of a more immediate predecessor, Fletcher. To portray love, Ford in four of his plays utilizes the same domestic situation: a husband's friend informs him that his wife has a lover and urges him to seek revenge. This similarity is noteworthy, yet implies a uniformity that does not exist; for example, two plays end in murder; two others, in reconciliation. Ford also champions courage; his characters die for love. While some of his women show Stoical resignation and others outspoken defiance, his four tragic heroes are of the same stamp, handsome and aggressive young men who scorn death.

Although Ford's own talent largely accounts for his literary achievement and is described at length in the following pages, he must also be viewed as a product of his times. As a dramatist, he is blessed with an extraordinary legacy, since the forty years preceding his plays constituted one of the richest literary eras in history. Ford uses this inheritance in many ways. At least three of his works show the influence of Shakespeare: *'Tis Pity* recalls *Romeo and Juliet;* *Love's Sacrifice, Othello;* and *Perkin Warbeck, Richard II. The Lover's Melancholy,* with its heroine disguised as a young man, is like the romantic comedies of Shakespeare and Fletcher. Domestic revenge, Ford's favorite story, appears in many an earlier drama. The prurient tone and surprise ending of *The Fancies* probably were suggested by Fletcher's similar practice; and the vivid, almost coarse, calumniation of sensuality found throughout Ford's works strongly resembles that in John Marston's. Our playwright also owes much to the Elizabethan theater, which had acquired by 1628 considerable professional competence. Performed by the King's Men and by Christopher Beeston's companies at the Phoenix,[2] his plays employ current theatrical techniques in their songs, dances, and tableaux. Ford's lovers, besides voicing their emotion, kneel and hold hands; Orgilus bleeds himself to death on stage; and Giovanni enters with his sister's heart on his dagger.

In addition, Ford is indebted to nondramatic literature. In *The Lover's Melancholy* and *The Broken Heart,* he uses Robert Burton's *The Anatomy of Melancholy,* and in *Perkin Warbeck,* Sir Francis Bacon's *History of the Reign of King Henry VII.* His many references to Platonism, Stoicism, and courtly love, though dependent upon no individual sources, also have literary origins. Finally, Ford is affected by the intellectual atmosphere of Caroline England, an environment not so exuberant and confident as that forty years earlier, and one that must partially explain his penchant for individualism, Stoicism, and, in one or two instances, morally questionable topics.

About Ford's life we have very little information. Because some of the writers of commendatory verses for his plays, as well as Ford himself, associate him with the Middle Temple— one of the Inns of Court, where young gentlemen received a general education—he is very likely the John Ford admitted there on November 16, 1602, as the second son of Thomas Ford of Ilsington, Devonshire.[3] The Fords were an established Devonshire family: the playwright's great-grandfather, John Ford of Ashburton, obtained a coat of arms in 1524; and the playwright's father owned one manor and part of another. Although Ford's birthdate is unknown, he was baptized at Ilsington on April 17, 1586. When at the Middle Temple, he was expelled in 1605/6 for failure to pay his buttery bill, and reinstated on June 10, 1608.

Upon his father's death in 1610, he was bequeathed ten pounds, an interesting fact in view of the greater amounts willed to his two younger brothers. It may reflect parental disapproval of his expulsion and of his first two literary ventures (both *Fame's Memorial* and *Honour Triumphant* were published in 1606). When his older brother, Henry, died in 1616, Ford was left twenty pounds a year for the rest of his life. In the next year, he was one of forty members of the Middle Temple reprimanded for wearing hats instead of lawyers' caps. Of the few contemporary references to Ford as a dramatist, most appear in Sir Henry Herbert's office book, in the Stationers' Register, and in the front matter of his plays. William Heminge, in his *Elegy on Randolph's Finger,* describes him along with a score of other writers: "Deep In a dumpe Iacke forde alone was gott/ With folded Armes and Melancholye hatt."[4] Thomas Heywood, in his *Hierarchie of Blessed Angels* (1635), explains he was nicknamed "Iacke"; Thomas Bancroft, in his *Two Bookes of Epigrammes and Epitaphs* (1639), devotes a two-line epigram to Ford; and the miscellany *Wits Recreations* (1640) contains another epigram about him.[5] After 1639 there is no certain record of the dramatist. The last play to be published with prefatory material by him, *The Lady's Trial,* appeared in that year. Shortly thereafter he probably either died or left London, but lack of evidence makes this hypothesis mere conjecture.

CHAPTER 2

Nondramatic Works

FORD's extant nondramatic writings, all published before his plays, consist of five works. Two of them—*Fame's Memorial* (1606) and *Christ's Bloody Sweat* (1613)—are poems; the other three—*Honour Triumphant* (1606), *The Golden Mean* (1613), and *A Line of Life* (1620)—are prose pamphlets. Ford's authorship of *Christ's Bloody Sweat* and *The Golden Mean* is probable rather than certain, but the two are now generally regarded as his. A sixth work, *Sir Thomas Overbury's Ghost* (1615), very likely in prose, is lost. Though not of great literary merit, these earlier pieces help to reveal Ford's development since they contain themes and attitudes depicted more fully, and masterfully, in his plays.

I Fame's Memorial

Fame's Memorial is an elegy on Charles Blount, Earl of Devonshire and eighth Lord Mountjoy, who died in 1606. The lengthy poem, dedicated by Ford to the Countess of Devonshire, is comprised of one hundred and twenty-eight seven-line iambic pentameter stanzas of laudatory biography, followed by nine short epitaphs or "Tombs" (associated by the author with the traditional Nine Worthies) and a one-hundred-and-twenty-line tenth "Tomb" that presents the earl as a tenth Worthy.[1] Ford was not the only author to voice praise: Samuel Daniel wrote another elegy, John Davies of Hereford and Joshua Sylvester had addressed sonnets to Lord Mountjoy, and Nicholas Breton had dedicated *The Honour of Valour* to him.[2]

Ford's frequent censure of detractors in *Fame's Memorial* was occasioned by the marriage of Lord Mountjoy to Lady Penelope Rich in 1605, a match that created considerable stir. In 1580, Penelope Devereux had been married against her will to Lord Rich; by 1586, Mountjoy probably was her lover, and after 1590 she became his mistress and bore him five children. When Lord Rich obtained an ecclesiastical divorce in 1602 or 1603, Mountjoy sought to wed Penelope, although canon law prohibited anyone divorced by ecclesiastical process from remarrying. When Lord Mountjoy persuaded William Laud, then his chaplain, to perform the marriage, doubts were raised as to its legality; and the king and queen, it is generally believed, were among those offended.

Ford's sympathy for the earl and his wife is even more evident in a manuscript version of the poem, probably the presentation copy and possibly in Ford's own hand, for the manuscript contains three stanzas not in the 1606 edition that strongly defend the countess; Bertram Lloyd suggests that the lines may have been omitted from the publications as a matter of prudence.[3] Concerning Penelope, we should note that, before her first marriage, she had been loved by Sir Philip Sidney, and is the Stella of his *Astrophel and Stella,* the famous sonnet sequence. One scholar, Stuart Sherman, believes that the frustrated love between Sidney and Penelope provided Ford with the germinal idea for one of his best plays, *The Broken Heart.*[4]

Because most of *Fame's Memorial* is biographical, some information about Mountjoy's career is necessary.[5] Born in 1563, the son of James, Lord Mountjoy, he attended Oxford for a short period, then studied law at the Inner Temple. When about twenty, he turned to the court, where his good looks made him a favorite of Queen Elizabeth. Although he and the Earl of Essex eventually became friends, the queen's bestowing of a golden chess piece upon young Mountjoy for his skill in a tilting match caused the jealous Essex to make an insulting remark; a duel ensued in which Essex was wounded. Mountjoy was knighted in 1586, and for the next seventeen years distinguished himself on the battlefield; he fought first in the Low Countries, then in Brittany, and in 1597 accompanied Essex to the Azores.

In 1598, Mountjoy became deeply involved with Essex and the Irish rebellion. In that year Hugh O'Neill, the Earl of Tyrone, routed the English forces. Mountjoy was expected to be appointed lord deputy, but Essex managed to secure the post. In 1599, however, when Essex was confined on suspicion of treason, Mountjoy replaced him. Mountjoy was implicated in some of Essex's plots; but the queen, needing his military leadership in Ireland, chose to ignore the evidence. In Ireland, Mountjoy was victorious, defeating Tyrone's army in 1601 and accepting the Irish leader's personal surrender in 1603. Returning to England in 1603 shortly after Elizabeth's death, he was created Earl of Devonshire by King James I; and he soon thereafter received several land grants.

Fame's Memorial, in its first eight stanzas, introduces its topic by means of a personification, Fame, who "soars now aloft triumphant" and "proclaims aloud defiance to disdain." Ford, in defending the earl and countess from their critics, shows his admiration for the aristocracy, for he associates "Fear" with peasants and servility "While haughty Fame adorns nobility,/ Planting her gorgeous throne upon the crest/ Of honour casquèd in a royal breast" (286). A similar attitude appears in some of his plays, principally in *The Broken Heart* and in *Perkin Warbeck,* both of which depict an aristocratic code of social poise and Stoical philosophy. The poem next refers to Mountjoy as Achilles and also, doubtless with the tenth "Tomb" in mind, as another Worthy. No poet can add to the earl's glory; had he been like Julius Caesar, he could have been the appropriate commentator on his own exploits.

After citing Mountjoy's friendship with Essex ("Thy soul's-united Essex"), Ford turns to biography. He briefly describes Mountjoy's education (289), then idealizes him as a courtier: "Here was he first who taught what should be done,/ How ladies should be lov'd, serv'd, woo'd, and won," for in his relationships he was neither "void of love's sense, nor yok'd in subjection/ Of servile passion" (291). In this part of the elegy, the stanza most relevant to Ford's dramas is that condemning hedonism; the evils of idleness and ease are described by characters in several plays, usually in connection with lust. The language, as well as the viewpoint, of the following lines is typical of later works:

> Let smooth-chinn'd amourists be cloy'd in play,
> And surfeit on the bane of hateful leisure,
> Let idle hours' follies youth betray,
> Unto the idle shame of boundless pleasure;
> Such petty apes of silk want reason's measure. (292)

Turning to the earl's military achievements, Ford reminds "forsaken soldiers" of their lost "Atlas." He cites the earl's soldiery in Belgium, praises his wife as an "angel . . . celestial," then tells "great Mountjoy's Irish story" (296–97). Leading his forces to victory, he was "treble-girt with force/ Of justice, force and valour" and "with sword and fire, void of a smooth remorse" (298). Yet he combined sternness with mercy, using both "words of milk and thunderbolts of brass." Thus, although Tyrone at his "very name didst quake," the Irish found him to be a restorer of peace and of prosperity: "Now they began to see, and seeing feel/ The sweet of concord. . . . A land of penury, scarcity, and want/ He hath enrich'd with plenty, ease, and store" (300–1). In Ford's English history play, *Perkin Warbeck,* Henry VII has similar capabilities; for, as he is subduing Warbeck and Cornish rebels, this able monarch shows both severity and mildness in meting out justice; and he continually strives for political and financial stability.

Then praising Mountjoy as counselor and statesman, Ford likens him to the king:

> As oft as James, the monarch of our peace,
> Shall be in after-chronicles recited,
> In that, to heaven's applause and subjects' ease,
> England and Scotland he in one united,
> A sight with which true Britons were delighted;
> So oft shalt thou eternal favour gain,
> Who recollectedst Ireland to them twain. (309)

Ford seems again to anticipate *Perkin Warbeck,* in which he portrays Henry VII as another uniter of nations; Henry, by marrying his daughter to the King of Scotland, initiated the eventual accession of James I to the English throne in 1603.

The remainder of *Fame's Memorial* presents, instead of biography, a series of panegyrical laments. One stanza (314), beginning "Life? ah, no life, but soon-extinguish'd tapers;/ Tapers? no tapers, but a burnt-out light!," has been mentioned by some scholars because of its likeness to Thomas Kyd's *The Spanish Tragedy,* but the stanza is not representative of the poem, which, on the whole, is lifeless in style.

II Honour Triumphant

Honour Triumphant: or the Peeres Challenge, also printed in 1606, is Ford's earliest prose work.[6] An appended poem, *The Monarches Meeting,* describes the occasion for the writing—the King of Denmark visited England in the summer of 1606—but is insignificant. In *Honour Triumphant,* dedicated to the Countess of Pembroke and to the Countess of Montgomery, Ford defends four "positions" championed by four nobles (the Duke of Lennox, the Earl of Arundel, the Earl of Pembroke, and the Earl of Montgomery) in a ceremonial challenge that welcomed the Danish monarch. The positions, "in honor of all faire Ladies," are that "Knights in ladies' service have no free-will," that "Beauty is the maintainer of valour," that "Fair lady was never false," and that "Perfect lovers are only wise." In an obvious bid for recognition and patronage, the author writes twenty-six pages of prose in which he defends each of the four assertions. With its labored rhetoric and facile argumentation, *Honour Triumphant* strives for cleverness rather than for conviction, an understandable aim in view of the circumstances. Nevertheless, some of the ideas and some of the language remind us of Ford's plays, most of which center on love.

In maintaining that "Knights in ladies' service have no free-will," Ford uses religious imagery like that in *The Broken Heart* and *Perkin Warbeck* to contend that "Women are saints above earth's paradise." He also phrases many of his arguments in the language of courtly love, a mode of speech to be found in the subplots of several of his plays: "Who can serve two masters? Who can be master of himself when he is a servant to his lady, but either he scorns the humility due to her, or affects a singularity to himself: if the one, he is no servant; if the other, an unfit lover" (348). As devoted "servants" he lists Paris, Troilus,

Aeneas, and Pelops; a fifth, contemporary one is probably
Mountjoy, described as "our English Hector, who [served] . . .
his never-sufficiently admired Opia [Penelope Devereux had become Lady Rich], a perfect Penelope to her ancient knight
Ulysses" (348–49).

Ford continues his display of verbal and logical ingenuity in
defending the second position, "Beauty is the maintainer of
valour." As an initial argument, he uses the early Romans, who
"violently seized upon the Sabines' ladies: by violence they won
them, by valour they justified their winning" (351). The captured ladies, continues the author, did their part by rewarding
Roman valor with Sabine kisses. Merchants and soldiers risk
their lives for the same reason; Hercules swam across the sea to
impress Deïanira; to be admired by ladies, kings enlarge em-
pires, courtiers polish their manners and cormorants hoard
treasure (355–56). Ignoring the fate of Marc Antony, Ford says
that, if Julius Caesar had been accompanied by Cleopatra, he
surely would have conquered Britain. And any "home-bred por-
ing academic" who charges that beauty makes a "warrior a flat
coward" the author dismisses as "an inexperienced plodder"
(357).

In supporting the third position, "Fair lady was never false,"
Ford begins by resorting to Aristotle's axiom that "The temperature of the mind follows the temperature of the body" (359).
Since nature is the "handmaid to heaven" and since beauty is the
"rarest workmanship" of nature, we must conclude that a beautiful lady is virtuous. In Ford's most sensational play, *'Tis Pity
She's a Whore,* Giovanni reasons somewhat similarly that nature
and beauty sanction incest between himself and his sister; but
he is rebuked for specious logic by a friar. In the final paragraph
of this third section (366), Ford distinguishes between *fair* and
lovely: "Every fair lady is lovely, but every lovely lady is not
fair: so then the lovely may be fickle, but the fair cannot be
inconstant." The unresolved problem, of course, is to decide
which of the two adjectives applies to any particular attractive
woman. But, even before this final escape clause, the author is
unworried, pressing more for wit than for wisdom. Thus, if a
person points out that some beautiful women have been unfaith-
ful, it can be answered that "Such abuse proceeds not from per-

fect beauty, but from that adulterate counterfeit of beauty,—
art" (360). In such a category belongs Helen of Troy, who
attracted men by her "inviting allurements" (361).

The fourth position, "Perfect lovers are only wise," is discussed in the shortest section of *Honour Triumphant*. A perfect
lover, claims Ford, needs "patience . . . to endure reproofs, wit
to procure content, boldness to attempt at opportunities" (368).
Love creates wisdom in two ways: the lover, by admiring such
beauty, gains more respect for its Creator and hence becomes
more devout; by acknowledging his inferior beauty, he grows
in humility. Ford concludes by extolling love in Platonic terms,
language that once again foreshadows that of his dramas:

Love is the only band, the alone obligation, that traffics betwixt earthly
creatures and heavenly angels, that unites woman to man, yea man to man,
nay man to himself, and himself to God. Love is the dignity of man's worth;
not a blind Cupid, a sensual lust, as poets feign, but an earnest and reasonable
desire of good, as authorities confirm. It is an entire conjunction of souls
together. (370)

Clifford Leech has called *Honour Triumphant* "a gallimaufry of
'platonic love,' mild sensuality, religious doctrine, and *amour
courtois*";[7] it is also an attempt at sophistication by a young
writer seeking recognition.

III Christ's Bloody Sweat

Christ's Bloody Sweat, a poem of approximately two thousand
lines, all in six-line stanzas, was published in 1613 with the
signature "I. F." on the title page and after the dedication.[8]
A. B. Grosart, in 1869, thought Joseph Fletcher to be the author,[9] but most scholars attribute the work to John Ford. Both
Joseph Hunter and J. P. Collier inclined to this view, which has
been more fully supported in this century by Joan Sargeaunt.[10]
Miss Sargeaunt thus summarizes her argument for Ford's authorship: "The dedication, written to one of his known patrons [the
Earl of Pembroke], in the style of his other dedications, is signed
'I. F.' There is one striking parallel (a passage of some length)
to a passage in *'Tis Pity*. The central idea of the poem is the one
religious idea that occurs with great frequency in Ford's plays.

The word 'pearl,' as always in Ford's verse, is dissyllabic. The
poem is written in the same manner and style as *Fames Memoriall*."[11]

The parallel to *'Tis Pity* consists of fourteen lines (26–27)
vividly describing the tortures suffered in Hell by the wanton,
the glutton, the murderer, the drunkard, and the miser; in the
drama, the friar so warns Annabella. Harold Oliver, however,
finds this likeness inconclusive since both passages could have
been derived separately from a similar one in Thomas Nashe's
Pierce Penniless.[12] Oliver does agree, on the other hand, that
the poem's theme of repentance appears in Ford's plays. In this
connection, both Oliver and Miss Sargeaunt give examples from
'Tis Pity and *The Broken Heart;* but they could have taken
others from *The Lady's Trial*, in which Levidolche tearfully renounces sin. The present consensus, in short, holds that *Christ's
Bloody Sweat* probably was written by Ford.

The title refers to the agony in Gethsemane, where, says the
author, Christ sweat blood in mental anguish and in compassion
for sinful man. The subject may have been suggested to Ford
by a similar poem, *Our Saviour's Passion* (c. 1600), written by
the Countess of Pembroke, to whom he had dedicated *Honour
Triumphant*.[13] The theme of *Christ's Bloody Sweat*, often repeated, is that tearful repentance will result, through the atone-
ment of Christ, in salvation. The writer more than once adds the
warning, however, that contrition should not be postponed until
the deathbed or even old age, for the sinner may discover that
he has become incapable of sincere repentance. To some extent,
the poem is Calvinistic and anti-Catholic, distinguishing between "the chosen, and elect" and "soules ordain'd to Hell"
(57) and attacking the Jesuits (55); but these comments come
late in the work, which emphasizes throughout man's opportunity to secure salvation by turning to Christ.

In the first four pages of *Christ's Bloody Sweat*, eight stanzas
relate that the spirit of Christ exhorted the author to write of
heavenly rather than of earthly matters. Later, to describe
Christ's invulnerability to lust, Ford attacks hedonism in language like that of *Fame's Memorial* and his plays:

     Lust could not traine his heart, or loue his eye,

> No wanton baites of pleasure could impawne
> His chast desire, to forfet to delight
> The lawelesse issues of a banefull night. (9)

After explaining that martyrs and the meek in spirit will be
saved whereas sinners will receive the just wrath of God (26–
36), Ford, speaking of love between man and woman, castigates
lust but praises conjugal love:

> But such whose lawfull thoughts, and honest heat,
> Doth temperately moue with chast desires,
> To choose an equall partner, and beget
> Like comforts by alike inkindled fires:
> Such find no doubt in vnion made so euen,
> Sweet fruits of succors, and on earth a heauen. (37)

This stanza is like the prothalamium that blesses the marriage
of Euphranea and Prophilus in *The Broken Heart;* such lines in
the poem and the play should not be ignored by scholars who
call Ford a champion of "free love."

To illustrate Christ's compassion, Ford presents Him as the
holy bridegroom courting the soul, "that Queen of Reason" (42–
47). The poet's use of the imagery of courtship for a religious
theme offers an interesting contrast to his plays, which frequently
describe human love in religious terms. "Ladie," begins Christ
the lover, "thy fortunes haue not won/ My heart to loue, thy
beauty cannot force mee/ To wanton dotage. . . . I craue,/ No
wanton dalliance in a bed of lust" (43). The soul accepts Christ
as her betrothed, but soon "like a strumpet false, she heere
forswore,/ That plighted promise," for she is seduced by "young
lust," who has that bawd, "old sin," persuade the soul not to
shun life's pleasures, since God surely will accept her later repentance (44). But Christ does not abandon the foolish soul,
and eventually she repents and is forgiven (47). The remainder
of the work deserves little attention, save possibly for thirteen
stanzas (59–61) which relate the life of Christ as someone might
describe it to a child. Having reiterated his theme of redemption,
Ford concludes by hoping that he has satisfactorily discharged
his "heauenly task" (62).

As art, *Christ's Bloody Sweat* is superior to Ford's other poem,

YEARY LIBRARY

LAREDO JR. COLLEGE

LAREDO, TEXAS

Fame's Memorial. A good number of its lines are not end-
stopped, thus avoiding the monotony of the earlier work. Its
rhetorical devices are well handled, and sometimes tie together
a series of stanzas; for example, twenty-one stanzas are connected by the phrases "here saw he" and "for them he sweated
blood" (11–15); five begin with "Doth any" (20–21); and six
are linked by means of identical terminal and initial lines (51–
52). Even more effective are several six-line similes: a sinner
saved by Christ is likened to a man rescued from a labyrinth
(15) and to a Christian merchant released from a Turkish galley
(16); Christ, to an actor (31); ephemeral man, to a "cunning
fire-work" (34)—a figure also used by Ithocles in *The Broken
Heart* (II.ii)—; angels to porters (38); and the bloody sweat to
a flooding river (56).

IV   The Golden Mean

Also published in 1613 was *The Golden Mean,* an anonymous
prose pamphlet described on its title page as *Lately written, as
occasion serued, to a great Lord. Discoursing The Noblenesse
of perfect Virtue in extreames.*[14] Although there is no dedication, a second edition (1614) states that the work was "formerly
written to the Earl of Northumberland," who was imprisoned in
the Tower of London at the time and who, in the first edition,
is discussed as a victim of "neglect" (69–70). Northumberland
also was the father-in-law of Viscount Doncaster, to whom Ford
dedicated the manuscript of *A Line of Life,* first printed in 1620.
A Line of Life, as has been shown by Miss Sargeaunt, provides
in its introduction the principal evidence for Ford's authorship
of *The Golden Mean:* "*In all things, no one thing can more re-
quisitely bee obserued to be practised, then* The Golden Meane:
*The exemplification whereof, however heretofore attributed, I
dare not so poorely under-value myselfe and labours, as not to
call mine.*"[15] As further proof, Oliver notes that another passage
in *A Line of Life* (manuscript version only) amounts to a summary of the earlier pamphlet;[16] and Robert Davril finds in *The
Golden Mean* several verbal parallels to lines in Ford's dramas.[17]
Hence, scholars now generally agree that Ford is the likely
author of *The Golden Mean.*

YEARY LIBRARY
LAREDO JR. COLLEGE
LAREDO, TEXAS

Like Bacon's essay "Of Adversity" (1625), *The Golden Mean* advocates Stoicism. That person is truly wise and noble who maintains his "moderation" in spite of disfavor (41–63), neglect (63–72), forfeit of estate (72–85), banishment (85–100), imprisonment (100–14), or death (114–26). Ford's topic is relevant not only to his era—many eminent persons besides Northumberland and Bacon suffered such hardships—but to his plays, especially *Perkin Warbeck*, in which the titular character resolutely accepts neglect, banishment, imprisonment, and death, and, to a considerable extent, *The Broken Heart*, in which three of the principals die stoically.

The first third of *The Golden Mean* (1–41) advocates a "prepared mind" equal to any emergency. Ford likens resolution to the sea, which neither rain nor flood nor wind nor tide can cause to "ouerflow with the rudenesse of passion" (5–6). Fear, whether in "the float of prosperitie" or "the ebbe of . . . plenty," is beneath the virtuous mind (7). At the same time, a wise man realizes he is a frail mortal, subject to mutability; he knows that in ancient times Pompey lost his wealth; Sejanus, his honors; and Ptolemy, his kingdoms (16); and that, more recently, Cardinal Wolsey and the Earl of Essex experienced similar reversals (17). Indeed, continues the writer, moral strength is best revealed by adversity, for "*A calme Sea and a faire Winde proues not a Sailers skill*" (19–20). And since life is but a perilous journey to death, "Nothing is left therefore to a man borne to liue, but a stayed and a sure resolution to be armed to die" (32). Avoiding both pride and servility, man should seek goodness rather than greatness (34). Without this philosophy, he is "carried by the violent streame of opinion" (36); with it, he has the stability of a "fixed Starre" (38), and, like a provident house builder, seeks "cures against the fates of extremitie" (40).

The remainder of *The Golden Mean* discusses the above-listed "Six Miseries that may befall a Noble man." The first, disfavor, results from private malice, "selfe-unworthynesse," envy, or "an vnguided Prince" (41–42). If a victim of malice, the noble person will be sustained by his retention of innocence and integrity (43–44). As for "selfe-unworthynesse"—whether ambition, discontent, covetousness, pride, faction, riot, or wantonness—the remedy is "selfe-reformation," which absolves even a penitent

robber of his past misdeeds (45–50); reformation may not regain
the prince's favor, but it restores self-respect. The victim of envy
has the consolation that his patience also frustrates his attackers,
that "it is better to be enuied then pittied" and that his true
worth has been found (52–57). Disfavor caused by a king's
inconstancy occurs so frequently that a man who relies upon a
prince's favor "is like a foolish Marchant that aduentures all his
substance in a broken vessell" (49–60).

Neglect, the second "misery" to be considered, may result from
a king's ingratitude or from his lack of discernment. In either
case, the recipient's peace of mind is easily maintained; for he
should perceive, in the former instance, that the ruler will go
down in history as "a dishonourable debtor" and, in the latter,
that recognition from a blind prince is as unlikely as thanks
from an ox or horse (63–66). An example of neglect, says Ford,
is Northumberland, who was speedily "disgraced of his Sou-
eraigne, forsaken of the Lords, and despised of the multitide"
(70). Withstanding such circumstances is the "just man . . . ,
whose soundnesse of minde like the Centre of the earth stands
euer vnmoued" (70).

The third extremity, "Forfeiture of Estate," is easily sustained
by a wise man, who attaches little importance to possessions.
Ford recalls the poor gardener who refused a kingdom offered
him by Alexander the Great (74). Concerning the loss of wealth,
either a man has earned it himself and hence is capable of re-
covering it, or he has inherited it without working and hence has
no legitimate complaint (76). Riches are to goodness and resolution as a light silk cloak is to warm furs. The former are superfluous vanities; the latter, necessities (77–78). In addition, wealth
often causes one "to hugge the loue of abundance, that he should
imagine the losse of it, should make him miserable" (84–85).

The fourth and fifth hardships are banishment and imprisonment, respectively. If banished for an evil deed, the offender
deserves his anguish, which his conscience, ever with him, will
provide (86–87). But the man exiled "vpon wrongfull or sleight
occasions" need not despair, for to "a noble and free resolution
. . . all Countryes are a home" (89). In fact, some, like Aeneas,
have voluntarily left their native lands to seek prosperity. Also,
a banished person can transform his apparent plight into a

"iourney of pleasure" by regarding himself as an ambassador to "some vnknowne Prince" (92–93). To a few, such banishment even has brought glory and power: Thomas Mowbray, Duke of Norfolk, having been so punished by Richard II, died fighting the Turks in Palestine and thereby gained the esteem of posterity (95–96); Henry of Richmond found "such fauour and loue in the Courts and hearts of forraine Princes" that he was able to defeat Richard III and become King Henry VII of England (97–98). And banishment induced greatness in Pompey, "counsell" in Scipio Africanus, courage in Hannibal, and wit in Ovid (98–99).

As for imprisonment, the resolute man triumphs over it. Turning to mythology, Ford likens the escaping Daedalus to spiritual freedom and the fallen Icarus to physical restriction (101–2). Prison affords time for reflection: "Men, accompanied with the imployment of worthy thoughts, are neuer less idle then when they are alone" (103–4). If the prisoner has books, he can make a virtue of necessity, for "The life of instruction is reading, and leisure the life of reading, and a retired restraint the life of leisure" (105). In addition, the imprisoned one discovers his true friends and grows in humility (113).

Death, the sixth and final "extreame," is actually "the onely remedie and securest ease against miserie" (114), for it ends all sorrows. Death is expected by the wise man and welcomed by the good one (115); poets have aptly compared it to night, which appears dark but gives rest (117–18). The person condemned to die may fear scandal, but he has the great advantage of being able to prepare himself for a noble death, whereas others "are many times suddenly taken in the fulnesse of their filthinesse" (119–20). Death, concludes Ford, is "a happy Hauen," "a safe Inne," "a path to blessednesse," and "a banquet of all goodnes" (121).

V A Line of Life

A Line of Life, a prose pamphlet by "Io. Ford," was printed in 1620.[18] Also extant is a manuscript copy (mentioned above in connection with *The Golden Mean*), probably by the same hand that penned *Fame's Memorial.* The handwriting may be

Ford's, or it may be that of a professional scribe; Oliver raises the latter possibility.[19]

Like *The Golden Mean*, *A Line of Life* advocates Stoicism; and it stresses the earthly "Immortalitie of a Vertuous Name." Yet it complements rather than repeats the earlier work; for, instead of dealing with life's extremities, it discusses action, "the crown of virtue" (388). To be laudable, action must display perseverance; perseverance, in turn, must display sufferance. Without these "three golden links," a man dies "without any issue to inherit his remembrance or commendation." Palm-readers, continues Ford, make much of the hand's so-called line of life; although such charlatans should not be heeded, says Ford, their phrase aptly describes his discourse on ethics (389). Throughout, Ford buttresses his arguments with numerous references to authorities. Seneca is cited the most often; among the others are Plato, Aristotle, Cicero, Horace, Pliny, Plutarch, and Augustine. But the pamphlet is not merely a pastiche of classical borrowings: the writer gives his own contemporary examples (Lord Harrington, Sir Walter Raleigh, the Earl of Essex, the Duke of Byron, Sir John van Olden Barnevelt, and King James I); and he also provides his own vivid analogies and metaphors.

A Line of Life contains three main parts, which discuss the proper conduct of "a man" (391–99), of "a public man" (399–409), and of "a good man" (409–16). Concerning the individual "man," since reason sets him above other creatures, he should emulate the "watchful providence" of God by intelligently ordering "the little world of himself" (392). Socrates has said that beauty of mind is more important than beauty of body. Yet intelligence without virtue is "like a diamond set in a rushen ring" (393); how easy it is "to gild a rotten post, to paint a sepulchre, to varnish an ill meaning" (394). Hypocrisy itself proves the value of goodness: without the latter, the former would have no reason for being.

Then, in a passage recalling *Fame's Memorial*, *Christ's Bloody Sweat*, and most of his plays, Ford once more attacks excessive pleasure: "We were not born to feed, sleep, and spin out our web of life in the delicate softness of vanity or sloth; we were not born to traffic in follies, and to make merchandise of our sensualities; we were not born to revel in the apishness of ridiculous expense of time; we were not born to be panders to that great whore of a declining reason, bewitching pleasure" (394–95). "Resolution" enables man to shun this "lethargy and disease of an infectious court-grace" and to lead a life "well worthy a chronicle—and chronicled will be in perpetual memory" (396). Standing alone, he will avoid "vanity [, which] most commonly rides coached in the highway, the beaten way, the common way."

Ford ends his first section with several ancient and modern instances of individual men ("not as they were commanders or employed for the commonwealth, but as they were commanders of their own infirmities"). He praises Epaminondas of Thebes, Phocion of Athens, and Brutus of Rome; from recent times he contrasts two: John, Lord Harrington, who "attained even in his youth not only to gravity in his behaviour, . . . but to perfection in his action" (398); and Sir Walter Raleigh, who, though "stored with the best of nature's furniture," was "subject to as many changes of resolution as resolute to be the instrument of change; politic, and yet in policy so unsteady, that his too much apprehension was the foil of his judgment" (399).

The "public man," discussed in the "second branch" of *A Line of Life*, is likened to "a blaze upon a mountain" and "a vigilant sentinel in a watch-tower," for he has great political responsibilities (399). Ford says he will not "dive into the depth of policy," since that would be as pretentious as Phormio lecturing to Hannibal on warfare, or Seneca to Nero on cruelty (400); on the other hand, a general approach to conduct needs no apology. Public men are beset by two principal evils: flattery and envy. Flattery is "the bawd to great men's shame, the nurse to their wantonness, the fuel to their lusts" (402). It is like a silken halter, soft but strangling; it is like the legendary panther, with sweet breath but cruel nature (403). As for the danger of envy, "men in high places are like some hopeless mariners set to sea in a leaking vessel" (405). If an Achilles has only one vulnerable heel, some "watchful Paris" will "wound his infirmity" (408). To illustrate what can befall public men, Ford cites contemporaries from England, France, and the Netherlands: the Earl of Essex, the Duke of Byron, and Barnevelt (406–7).

The last section of *A Line of Life* deals with the "good man" who looks after others as well as himself. He leads a life of action, remembering that God is the "rewarder of adverbs, not of nouns" (409). Sometimes his frankness procures hatred rather than friendship, but ingrates do not realize that "the healthfulest medicines smart most in the wound" (411). Though he is defamed and traduced, "his own solace is to him . . . an unexpugnable castle. . . . his integrity to him is a brazen wall" (412–13). All kings, of course, are public men; but those who help neighboring countries—"repressing of hostilities, enlarging a confederacy, confirming an amity, settling a peace, supplanting an heresy"—are also good men. Such a king is James I, "who hath thus long sought . . . to decide, discuss, conclude, and determine all differences between his neighbouring princes and fellows in Europe" (414); he should be called "James the Good" (415). In this section, as well as in a three-page epilogue which echoes *The Golden Mean* in a paragraph devoted to noble suffering in adversity, Ford points towards *Perkin Warbeck*, where Henry VII, like James I, strives for peace among nations and where Warbeck, his antagonist, rises in dignity as his fortune falls.

Ford's nondramatic writings, while having some intrinsic worth, in no way match his plays; their chief importance today is the light they shed on his subsequent literary career. One conclusion to be drawn from them is growth. That is, *Christ's Bloody Sweat* (1613) is better poetry than *Fame's Memorial* (1606), and *The Golden Mean* (1613) and *A Line of Life* (1620) are better prose than *Honour Triumphant* (1606), though in fairness to a fledgling author, it must be admitted that he is somewhat the victim of his first two topics: an elegy for an earl, and a defense for courtly charades. A second conclusion is that continuity in both theme and language marks Ford's entire output. Love, beauty, fame, antihedonism, repentance, Stoicism, and able kingship appear both in his nondramatic and in his dramatic works.

CHAPTER 3

Collaborations and The Queen

BETWEEN 1620 and 1628, the year *The Lover's Melancholy*, probably his first unaided play, was licensed, Ford collaborated with other dramatists; but for various reasons the nature and extent of this apprenticeship are hard to determine. We do know that he wrote *The Witch of Edmonton* (acted in 1621) with Dekker and Rowley; *The Sun's Darling* (licensed in 1624) with Dekker; *The Fairy Knight* (licensed in 1624) with Dekker; *A Late Murther of the Son upon the Mother* (licensed in 1624) with Dekker, Webster, and Rowley; and *The Bristowe Merchant* (licensed in 1624) with Dekker.[1] Unfortunately, of these five plays only *The Witch of Edmonton* and *The Sun's Darling* are extant, although the licensing of the other three dramas helps to confirm Ford's literary activity around 1624 and his close association with Dekker, an experienced playwright.

The two surviving works, especially *The Sun's Darling*, present some problems. *The Witch of Edmonton* was not published until 1658; but, so far as is known, this edition is the original version. Scholars' ascription of various scenes to Ford, Dekker, or Rowley depends upon internal evidence that is discussed below. *The Sun's Darling*, licensed in 1624 and first printed in 1656, probably was revised (by Ford or by someone else) in 1638 or 1639, in which case the task of ascertaining Ford's contribution becomes all the more arduous.

Ford may also have written or helped to write plays that do not bear his name. From Humphrey Moseley in 1660 to Alfred Harbage in 1940, such claims have been made, usually on the

basis of internal evidence.² Of these, by far the most generally
accepted today is Ford's authorship of the anonymous *The
Queen* (first printed in 1653). The other attribution usually
acknowledged, though with more reservations, is his authorship
of all or part of *The Spanish Gypsy*, licensed in 1623 and published in 1653 as by Middleton and Rowley. Considering the
above facts and conjectures, it seems wisest to treat this part of
Ford's career by discussing only those plays most usually accepted as partially or wholly written by Ford: *The Witch of
Edmonton*, *The Sun's Darling*, *The Spanish Gypsy*, and *The
Queen*.

I The Witch of Edmonton

The Witch of Edmonton,³ still admired and often antholo-
gized, almost certainly was written in 1621; for in that year its
source, *The Wonderfull Discoverie of Elizabeth Sawyer A Witch
Late of Edmonton*, by Henry Goodcole, was printed and the
play itself was performed in December at Whitehall. Although
scholars have disagreed as to which parts Ford wrote, most of
them believe that his contribution is considerable, perhaps the
greatest. Thus as early as 1621 he was, it seems, extensively
involved in creating a first-rate drama. This likelihood affords a
useful approach to Ford's literary evolution, for an examination
of *The Witch of Edmonton* with his subsequent plays in mind
reveals directions he later took and others that he ignored.

The story of *The Witch of Edmonton* consists of two plots,
that of Mother Sawyer and that of Frank Thorney, Winnifrede,
and Susan Carter. The former is usually attributed to Dekker,
the latter to Ford; Rowley is given credit for some comical
scenes between the devil, who appears as Mother Sawyer's dog,
and Cuddy Banks, a clownish rustic. The titular character is an
old woman whose neighbors so frequently, but falsely, accuse
her of witchcraft that she offers her soul to the devil in order to
obtain revenge. The devil, who comes to her in the form of a
black dog, brings about various misfortunes to her persecutors;
but he abandons her as she is sentenced to death as a witch.
Frank Thorney, son of an Edmonton gentleman, has secretly
wed Winnifrede, a servant girl; but, when his father tells him
that, to keep his inheritance, he must marry Susan Carter, daugh-

ter of a rich yeoman, he does so. Planning to run off with Winnifrede and the money, Frank kills the virtuous Susan, wounds
himself, and accuses two other men of the crime. Susan's sister,
Katherine, discovers the murder weapon, and Frank is caught.
Before his execution, he remorsefully repents and is forgiven.

Although Ford probably contributed much more to the Thorney plot than to the Sawyer one, he surely was familiar with
and hence later influenced by the entire play. This point is usually overlooked; it is even possible, for instance, that those parts
of *The Witch of Edmonton* most resembling his own dramas
were written by Dekker or Rowley, his two collaborators. And
surely the work's skillful construction made a lasting impression.
Both plots have the theme of damnation and are overtly linked
by the devil dog. The dog is more prominent in the scenes with
Mother Sawyer and Cuddy Banks, speaking to both of them,
but also functions significantly in Thorney's crime. Immediately
before Frank and Susan enter (III.iii), the dog says, "The mind's
about it now; one touch from me/ Soon sets the body forward";
a few lines later, when it rubs against Frank, he at once decides
upon murder. Following the crime, the dog helps Frank tie
himself to a tree; in Act IV, it dances joyfully in anticipation of
Katherine's finding of the fatal dagger, and it later paws softly
at Frank as Katherine whispers the discovery to her father. Another linking device is Mother Sawyer. In a scene occurring
between Susan's murder and Frank's exposure, she responds to
the epithet of "witch" by asking "Who is not?" and she describes, at length, lecherous women, prodigals, shrews, corrupt
lawyers, and, finally and pertinently, "men-witches," who seduce
innocent maids and "put counterfeit pieces/ Away for true
gold" (IV.i). In Act V, when old Carter asserts that Frank
could not have murdered Susan "without the devil," she replies,
"Who doubts it? But is every devil mine?"

Effective also are the play's characterization and dialogue.
Mother Sawyer seems more awesome than pitiful in her resentment of malice (II.i), in her indictment of society (IV.i), and
in her lust for revenge, when she berates the devil, now a white
dog to signify her imminent death:

> Why to mine eyes art thou a flag of truce?
> I am at peace with none; 'tis the black colour,

> Or none, which I fight under: I do not like
> Thy puritan paleness; glowing furnaces
> Are far more hot than they which flame outright. (V.i)

Frank Thorney's duplicity concerning Susan is expertly depicted in evasive answers to his suspicious father:

OLD THORNEY. You love her, do you not?
FRANK.   'Twere pity, sir,
       I should deceive her.
OLD THORNEY.   Better you'd been unborn.
       But is your love so steady that you mean,
       Nay, more, desire, to make her your wife?
FRANK.   Else, sir,
       It were a wrong not to be righted. (I.ii)

Dialogue becomes powerfully ironic when Susan entrusts her departing husband to his other wife, Winnifrede, who is disguised as a boy; and in the final scene dialogue evokes our pity as Frank repents and is forgiven by Susan's father and his own.

The respective contributions of Ford, Dekker, and Rowley cannot be determined precisely; indeed, the assumption that any given scene was written by only one man may be questioned. Nevertheless, some lines closely resemble those in Ford's other dramas and thus suggest his authorship. H. Dugdale Sykes, who has found many verbal parallels to the works of both Ford and Dekker, has concluded that of the play's twelve scenes Ford wrote three (I.i, III.ii, and V.ii); Dekker, one (IV.i); Rowley, none; and Ford and Dekker together, four.[4]

Besides containing the similarities in language to Ford's other dramas noted by Sykes, *The Witch of Edmonton* foreshadows Ford's later work in more general ways; and, if we are concerned not with distinguishing among the three authors but with viewing the whole play as formative, these broader similarities become noteworthy. For example, the introductory "argument" that "Forc'd marriage, murder; murder blood requires" describes the theme of *The Broken Heart*. Again, the reconciliation between Thorney and old Carter (V.ii) is, as Oliver has pointed out,[5] like that between Warbeck and Huntley in the last act of *Perkin Warbeck*; but we should add that the similarity is more

extensive because earlier in both plays Carter (I.ii) and Huntley
(I.ii) good-naturedly see their daughters being wooed (unsuc-
cessfully) and apply the same proverb, "Win 'em and wear 'em."

The characterization of Susan prefigures that of Penthea in
The Broken Heart. The pitiless Thorney calls Susan "whore,"
explains he is already married, then stabs her; Susan replies,
"Die? O, 'twas time!/ How many years might I have slept in
sin,/ [The] sin of my most hatred [*sic*] too, adultery?" (III.iii).
Penthea offers the same kind of poignancy, but it extends through
several acts, dominating *The Broken Heart.* Pure and selfless
like Susan, she has been forced to marry Bassanes, though previously betrothed to the man she loves, Orgilus; as a result, she,
too, regards her marriage as adulterous, calls herself "whore,"
and welcomes death. In addition, repentance (Thorney's) and its
forgiveness become a theme of both the main and secondary
plots of *The Lady's Trial;* and if, as most commentators believe,
Ford did write this scene about Thorney, then his earlier poem,
Christ's Bloody Sweat, probably influenced him, since it stresses
sin, contrition, and forgiveness.

II The Sun's Darling

The Sun's Darling was licensed on March 3, 1624, as "a masque
by Deker, and Forde,"[6] but was not printed until 1656. Several
decades ago, some scholars contended that the work was a revision by Ford of Dekker's lost play *Phaethon,* written in 1598;
but today this hypothesis is generally rejected on the grounds
that, although Raybright, the masque's protagonist, is a child of
the sun, his actions have nothing to do with the Phaeton myth.[7]
Thus *The Sun's Darling* probably was not written before 1623.
It may have been revised, however, in 1638 or 1639, for the first
part of Act V obviously digresses from the rest of the play and,
as W. W. Lawrence has suggested,[8] probably refers to the difficulties Charles I was having with Scotland and to his proposed
trip there at that time. Gerald Bentley also notes that in 1639
William Beeston claimed the masque for his repertory at the
Phoenix theater and wonders if the producer's interest might
not have been aroused in part by the current appeal of such
political revisions.[9]

How much of *The Sun's Darling,* then, is Ford's? If, as is

likely, the play was revised in 1638 or 1639, how much was it
altered, and by whom? Ford could have been the reviser, but
there is no way of knowing. On the other hand, only the passage
in Act V is obtrusive; the remainder of the work is unified and
probably most, if not all, of it was composed by Ford and Dekker around 1623. Using this premise, Sykes and Sargeaunt have
attempted to divide the work between the two playwrights on
the basis of style; but Oliver finds their conclusions unconvincing.[10] As in the case of *The Witch of Edmonton,* another, and
very important, consideration has often been ignored: around
1623 Ford collaborated on *The Sun's Darling* with Dekker, so
later he must have been familiar with and influenced by the
entire work; very likely most of the 1656 edition consists of the
original version; and thus an examination of this masque gives
us a better understanding of Ford's development as a playwright.

The plot may be summarized briefly. Raybright, "the Sun's
darling," seeks to cure melancholy by abandoning dreams and
"fantasy" for the delights of nature. Upon the advice of the Sun,
he visits the garden of Spring, where he is attended by Youth,
Health, and Delight. But Raybright, introduced by the squire
Folly to the seductress Humour, craves variety in pleasure and
so forsakes these natural blessings. He goes to the court of Summer and is entertained by Plenty; then once again he is persuaded to leave by his two foolish companions. The same thing
happens at the court of Autumn, and Raybright turns to the
court of Winter, where the Sun censures him for the foolishness
and vanity of his life.

The title page of *The Sun's Darling* calls it "a moral masque."
The epithet is well chosen, for, as H. K. Russell has shown, the
work combines two dramatic genres: the morality play and the
masque.[11] The former is evident in both plot and characterization. Raybright is an Everyman who rejects the blessings of his
heavenly father; the four seasons and their attendants are de-
scendants of the Virtues and the good angels, while Folly and
Humour are quite like the traditional Vices. The moral, stressed
throughout, is that man, whether young, middle-aged, or old,
should be guided by reason and enjoy the natural gifts of life;
if, distracted by folly and "humour," he craves constant variety
in pleasure, he will never find contentment.

The masque characteristics appear in the play's many songs and dances. Act I has three songs, and each of the remaining four acts (one for every season) has a song and a dance. In Act V, eight masquers enter not only to sing and dance but to underline the Sun's final pronouncement that he who partakes wisely of pleasure will, because of the harmony of the "four Elements" and "four Complexions" within him, have good health; for the eight figures are none other than Earth, Air, Fire, and Water and Phlegm, Blood, Choler, and Melancholy. In addition, cornets, recorders, and oboes are played; and there are frequent musical flourishes.

Concerning the influence of *The Sun's Darling* on Ford's later dramas, we find interesting relationships in both theme and technique. The masque's theme deals with wise and foolish pleasures; in each season, Raybright must choose between them, and both alternatives are advocated by other personae. This pattern of ethical conflict appears in some of Ford's tragedies: in *'Tis Pity,* the principal tension is between incest and "Heaven's positions"; in *Love's Sacrifice,* between physical consummation and Platonic abstinence. Critics have disagreed about Ford's point of view in these two later plays, and their debates are discussed in subsequent chapters. Nevertheless, we may claim at this point both Ford's indebtedness and his inventiveness in regard to *The Sun's Darling*: he takes the general structure of the earlier work and subsequently uses it to depict different, and more tragic, moral issues. Also, we should mention some specific thematic similarities to other plays: Raybright's melancholy in Act I becomes the central story of *The Lover's Melancholy,* in which Prince Palador and Meleander are cured of the same illness; and the masque's first song, as well as the Sun Priest's advice to Raybright, is like Ithocles's speech in *The Broken Heart* (IV.i), when he argues for "A real, visible, material happiness" (i.e., marriage to Princess Calantha) as opposed to the vain fancies of dreams.

The Sun's Darling anticipates Ford's later work in several other ways. *The Broken Heart* contains four songs, the lyrics of which recall the above-mentioned song on Raybright's melancholy, and Calantha's court dance in Act V of the same tragedy owes something to masque dramaturgy. Masques occur in *Perkin Warbeck*

(III.ii), 'Tis Pity (IV.i), Love's Sacrifice (III.iv), and The Lover's Melancholy (III.iii). In Perkin Warbeck, the masque is not vital to the plot, being simply entertainment at the court of King James IV of Scotland: four of Warbeck's counselors enter as "wild Irish" and dance with four of James's attendants, who are dressed as "Scotch antics." In 'Tis Pity, masked ladies dance at the wedding feast of Soranzo and Annabella; then one of them unmasks to reveal herself as Hippolita, the bridegroom's former mistress. In Love's Sacrifice, the masque functions more significantly, occasioning the death of the lustful Ferentes: three women he has seduced dance around him, fatally stab him, then present as justification their infants, whom he has sired.

In The Lover's Melancholy, the physician Corax uses a masque to help cure Prince Palador of melancholy: several masquers appear, one at a time, to represent various kinds of neurosis; when no one enters to portray love melancholy, it becomes obvious that Palador himself exhibits it. This masque could have been suggested to Ford by the final one in The Sun's Darling, which also is concerned with peace of mind, though by means of harmonized "Elements" and "Complexions." Although Ford would have known about masques and morality plays if he had never helped to write The Sun's Darling, his collaboration with Dekker gave him firsthand experience with the two genres early in his career and partially accounts for his later utilization of them.

III   The Spanish Gypsy

Ford's name appears on the title pages of both The Witch of Edmonton and The Sun's Darling, but not on those of the next two plays to be discussed, The Spanish Gypsy (licensed in 1623 and printed in 1653 and 1661 as by Middleton and Rowley) and the anonymous The Queen (printed in 1653), both of which have been attributed to Ford by twentieth-century scholars solely on the basis of style. With such limited evidence, we hesitate to examine the latter dramas as influences on Ford's later work, and we are inclined to concentrate, instead, on the question of his alleged authorship. Commentators on Ford now regard The Queen as almost certainly his and, in effect, add it to the canon as an eighth unaided play; there is less unanimity, however, about his participation in *The Spanish Gypsy*. I share this prevailing attitude, since I see in Ford's works many more similarities, both specific and general, to *The Queen.*

The first scholar to assign *The Spanish Gypsy* to Ford was Sykes, who in 1924 cited verbal parallels; according to Sykes, the entire play is Ford's and could not have been written by Middleton and Rowley because it is not in their style.[12] In 1935, Sargeaunt supported Sykes's view, except for the Gypsy scenes.[13] Oliver, however, finds their evidence "both less convincing and harder to interpret than in [*The Witch of Edmonton*]" and also notes that Middleton's authorship has been defended by Una Ellis-Fermor, who sees a strong similarity between Clara's plight and that of Bianca in *Women Beware Women,* and by W. D. Dunkel, who asserts that even the comic scenes are not unlike those in Middleton's other plays.[14] Thus it seems sufficient merely to summarize briefly *The Spanish Gypsy* and then mention those parts that to some scholars suggest Ford's hand.

The story consists of two plots, both taken from Cervantes's *Exemplary Novels.* In one, Lord Alvarez, banished for having slain the father of Louis de Castro, disguises himself and his family as Gypsies and remains in Spain. Don John, a young nobleman who has fallen in love with Constanza, Alvarez's niece, is falsely accused of theft. Alvarez identifies himself in order to save the youth, and this unselfish act so impresses Louis that he forsakes revenge and is reconciled with Alvarez. In the other plot, one more serious in tone, Roderigo abducts, ravishes, then dismisses Clara, neither one learning the other's name. Later remorseful, he joins the "Gypsies" as a scholar. Clara, by chance visiting his home (where the rape took place), realizes that it is Roderigo who has wronged her and tells his father. The latter, not deceived by his son's disguise, arranges for his marriage to Clara, with whom Roderigo has fallen in love but whom he does not recognize as his former victim. After the wedding, Roderigo learns the truth and is properly repentant and happy.

The language and characterization of *The Spanish Gypsy* at times recall Ford's plays, but much less than *The Queen* does. Sykes and Sargeaunt see in the unusual contraction *d'ee* a significant verbal parallel. They, and some others, also find in the portrayals of Clara and Constanza an extolling of feminine virtue similar to that in Fordian drama. The playwright may have been responsible for all or part of *The Spanish Gypsy*, but to me such a hypothesis seems insufficiently documented.

IV The Queen

The anonymous *The Queen, or the Excellency of her Sex,* published in 1653, is now generally regarded as Ford's. In 1906, W. Bang listed numerous verbal parallels and briefly pointed out similarities in action, characterization, and ideas;[15] Sherman (1908), Sykes (1924), and Sargeaunt (1935) have provided additional support for Bang's position.[16] However, I hesitate to accept Ford's authorship without any reservation, simply because no external evidence supports it; moreover, I shall utilize *The Queen* very little in discussing his seven principal plays, as I do not want to base analysis upon a questionable premise. Yet having closely studied all of Ford's works, I must confess that *The Queen* does strike me as his; and I offer additional evidence to support this view.

The story is set in Aragon, where Alphonso, who led an unsuccessful rebellion against the queen, has been sentenced to death. But the queen, falling in love, offers him life and marriage. As soon as the wedding takes place and Alphonso is named king, he banishes from his presence, first for a week, then indefinitely, his wife, who dutifully obeys him. Meanwhile, the queen's general, Velasco, courts the widow Salassa and, to prove his love, states he will do whatever she wishes; Salassa promptly commands the warrior to refuse to fight, no matter what the provocation, and to give no reason for his inaction. As for King Alphonso, Muretto (his adviser) convinces him that the queen is having an affair with Petruchi, a young lord. Alphonso becomes furiously jealous; he also becomes aware of his wife's great beauty. In an emotional dilemma, he accuses her of adultery and decides that her honor will be tried by combat. Alphonso himself will meet any champion who may defend her; if none appears, she will be executed.

When the queen's counselors offer one hundred thousand

ducats for a champion, Salassa offers to release Velasco from his vow, but he scornfully rejects her proposal and charges her with avarice. Salassa, condemned to die for her failure to aid the queen, realizes she loves Velasco and penitently awaits her death. When she is on the scaffold, her execution is halted by Velasco, who, though still disdainful, terminates his vow of in-action to save her life. He next appears as the queen's champion, despite her command that he not challenge Alphonso. Velasco is followed by two more champions: Petruchi, who swears the queen is innocent, and Muretto, who reveals that his reports of the queen's infidelity have been falsehoods, told to arouse the king's jealousy and love. All ends happily as the king and queen declare their love and as Velasco, forgiving Salassa, asks her to marry him.

Bang, in attributing *The Queen* to Ford, depends chiefly on verbal parallels. Some of these are unconvincing because they are conventional and hence common to all Elizabethan drama. Others, however, point to Ford. To cite three of Bang's many examples, "This same whorson Court diet . . . and ease, have addicted me . . . to the touch of concupiscence" (1023ff.) is like "This same whoreson court-ease is temptation/ To a rebel-lion in the veins" in *The Broken Heart* (II.ii); "my words and thoughts are twins" (1393) is like "My tongue and heart are twins" in *The Broken Heart* (III.iii) and like "So martyrdom and holiness are twins" in *The Lover's Melancholy* (IV.iii); and "I'le kneel to thee, as to another nature" (3456) is like "Create me what you please of yours; do this,/ You are another nature" in *The Fancies* (I.i) and like "Mistery there, like to another nature,/ Confects the substance of the choicest fruits" in *The Sun's Darling* (IV.i). I should like to add two others to Bang's list: "A lady, yet . . . a popingjay. . . . A Wagtail is a glorious fowl in respect of many of ye" (851ff.) is like "How they flut-ter,/ Wagtails and jays together" in *The Broken Heart* (II.i), and "The flight of my ambitions soars no higher,/ Then living in your grace" (1440–41) is like "You . . . instruct/ Ambition not to soar a farther flight/ Than in the perfum'd air of your soft voice" in *Perkin Warbeck* (I.ii).

The Queen also reminds us of Ford's other plays in less spe-cific but nonetheless significant ways. S. Blaine Ewing, Jr., has claimed that both it and *The Lover's Melancholy* are indebted to Burton's *The Anatomy of Melancholy:* the former drama for its depiction of misogyny, the latter for its depiction of melancholy.[17] There are additional similarities between the two plays. The Salassa-Velasco subplot parallels the Thamasta-Menaphon one in *The Lover's Melancholy:* in each, a proud and beautiful lady, wooed in the language of courtly love, haughtily treats her abject suitor yet eventually experiences humility and love. The railing between Muretto and Pynto (an astronomer) is like that between Corax and Rhetias: both scenes appear in the first act, and both seem irrelevant to their respective stories, functioning mainly to enliven the otherwise decorous language of two tragicomedies. The successive entries of Velasco, Petruchi, and Muretto as the queen's champions in Act V have a counterpart in those of Aretus, Amethus, Sophronos, and Eroclea in effecting the cure of Meleander in *The Lover's Melancholy*—though, in this respect, *The Broken Heart* provides a greater likeness, since Calantha reacts to the three interruptions of the dance (by Armostes, Bassanes, and Orgilus) with an aristocratic hauteur similar to that of Alphonso's queen.

The Queen also echoes other Ford plays. Muretto's rousing of Alphonso's jealousy, as well as Alphonso's resultant ambivalence toward his wife, recalls the main story of *Love's Sacrifice*. The play's Stoicism—Alphonso, Salassa, and the queen resolute on the scaffold; Velasco patient in his physical humiliation—reminds us of Warbeck in the stocks (*Perkin Warbeck*) and of Ithocles in the fatal chair (*The Broken Heart*). And the spectacle of Alphonso on his throne, with Petruchi and the queen seated on either side, symbolizes the king's inner conflict just as the sedentary grouping of Ithocles, Orgilus, and Penthea in *The Broken Heart* visualizes that trio's fatal bond. Bufo (a braggart soldier) is reproached by Herophil (the queen's attendant) in the same way that Groneas and Hemophil are ridiculed by Christalla and Philema in *The Broken Heart*. The repentance of Salassa, as well as the vitriolic language rebuking her and the supposedly adulterous queen, is typical of several plays. In short, *The Queen* seems Ford's for many reasons.

Davril mentions as a probable source *The Dumb Knight* (1608) by Machin and Markham.[18] In it, the Salassa-Velasco subplot becomes central. Philocles, favorite of the King of Cyprus, wins Sicily and its queen for his monarch by defeating her two champions. Then, in a scene quite similar to one in *The Queen*, Philocles courts Mariana, who tells him to show his love by becoming speechless. When the king is upset by the apparent malady of his friend, Mariana confidently promises to cure him, but is unsuccessful. Consequently sentenced to death, she is saved by Philocles, who ends his silence but at the same time, like Velasco, condemns her both for imposing a cruel task and for causing him to break a vow. Philocles also states that he will accept Mariana only if she proves her love for him, and she does so in the remainder of the story. Her brother, Epire, hating Philocles, convinces the king that the queen and Philocles are lovers. When Philocles is sentenced to death, Mariana visits him in prison and the two exchange clothes, enabling Philocles to escape and to appear as his own champion. He defeats Epire in single combat, the latter confesses, and all ends happily.

Ford's alteration of his apparent source requires some comment. He subordinates the "dumb knight" story and expands the relationship between king and queen; probably influenced by Burton (Davril also cites several contemporary works indicting women),[19] he makes misogyny and its cure central; and, to this end, he converts the vengeful Epire into the crafty but benevolent Muretto. He also ties his two stories together more skillfully by contrasting the misogynist king and doting queen with the servile Velasco and haughty Salassa; by inducing amorous passion in the king and contrite love in Salassa; and, in the final act, by bringing both the queen and Salassa to the scaffold, where they are saved by the same champion, Velasco.

Despite structural superiority to *The Dumb Knight*, *The Queen* is not one of Ford's better plays. Sharing with *The Lover's Melancholy* an interest in Burtonian psychology, it presents the subject less artfully. The curing of Palador and Meleander by Corax is gradual, plausible, and esthetically appealing (see Chapter 4); Alphonso's sudden realization of his wife's beauty is inadequately motivated; and Muretto's role as physician is not disclosed to us until the last scene. These differences suggest that *The Queen*, if Ford's, is earlier, and that he profited from

it in *The Lover's Melancholy*. There are further weaknesses,
most of them in areas handled more expertly in other plays.
The queen is a passive figure until the fifth act, when she displays some mettle in censuring the three champions who pre-
sume to challenge the king; Calantha in *The Broken Heart*
demonstrates regal decorum much more effectively. The vow-
inhibited Velasco comes perilously close to comedy when sub-
mitting to the blows of the braggart Bufo; Bassanes in *The
Broken Heart*, when he eagerly participates in the bloodletting
of Orgilus, is a superior exemplar of inordinate Stoicism. Bufo
and the comic astronomer Pynto, though using colorful language, are relevant to the plot only in the denouement, when
their punishment for immorality signifies that Alphonso's previous companionship with them has somehow accounted for his
misogyny; Ford does much better in *Perkin Warbeck*, in which
Warbeck's quartet of ludicrous advisers serve throughout the
play to undercut their leader's political stature without dimin-
ishing his personal dignity.

Of the four plays discussed in this chapter, only *The Witch of
Edmonton* and *The Sun's Darling*, because external evidence
argues Ford's hand in them, are reliable guides to his literary
apprenticeship. Containing many elements that reappear in his
mature work, they reveal his growth as a playwright. Thorney's
enforced marriage and his eventual repentance in *The Witch of
Edmonton*, for example, become major themes in *The Broken
Heart* and *The Lady's Trial*, respectively, while the masque
devices in *The Sun's Darling* are turned into vehicles for tragedy
in *The Broken Heart* and *Love's Sacrifice*. In this respect, *The
Spanish Gypsy* and *The Queen* are less helpful. The former is
licensed early enough (1623), but the names of Middleton and
Rowley on the title page cannot be ignored; and the story and
characterizations bear no pronounced similarity to Ford's plays.
As for *The Queen*, its anonymous authorship and late printing
(1653) must be reckoned with; yet the work does contain many
likenesses to Fordian drama, especially *The Lover's Melancholy*,
to which we now turn.

CHAPTER 4

Psychotherapy as Spectacle:
The Lover's Melancholy

I *The Story and Its Sources*

OF the seven extant plays written solely and unquestionably
by Ford, four are tragedies and three are tragicomedies.
Critics have always shown a marked preference for the former,
an attitude probably warranted by the excellence of *The Broken
Heart* and *'Tis Pity She's a Whore;* but the preference has resulted in the undeserved neglect of one tragicomedy, *The Lover's
Melancholy.*[1] Two other causes for the oversight are the work's
use of Burton's *The Anatomy of Melancholy* and its dates of
licensing (1628) and publication (1629). The fact that in a few
instances Ford closely follows *The Anatomy* does not mean his
entire play is modeled on it, yet some commentators imply it is
by their preoccupation with Burton's well-known work.

As for the drama's licensing and publication, because they
precede by several years the next earliest known date for any
of Ford's six other plays (1633), scholars have tended to regard
The Lover's Melancholy as his first unaided drama and hence
to minimize it as a precursor of greater things instead of considering it, as a work of art, in terms of itself. Even if *The
Lover's Melancholy* were without doubt the earliest, such an
approach would be dubious. But the chronology of Ford's plays
is very indefinite; some may have been written before the tragicomedy. Of one thing we can be sure: whenever Ford did write

this drama, he was a very competent artist, presenting in his main plot—six scenes in which the melancholy of Prince Palador and Lord Meleander is diagnosed and cured—psychotherapy as spectacle.

Analysis of *The Lover's Melancholy* requires a summary of its story. Prince Palador, the ruler of Cyprus (his father, King Agenor, having died), suffers from melancholy; the cause of his malady, as he admits to a confidant, is the loss of Eroclea, who, though contracted to marry him, was wooed by his late father and then mysteriously "conveyed away," never to be heard of again. Also grief-stricken is Eroclea's father, Lord Meleander, whose distracted outbursts require constant attendance.

To this rather despondent court there returns from Greece the young Lord Menaphon, who is anxious to see his beloved Thamasta, a proud beauty and cousin of Prince Palador. Menaphon brings with him a stranger named Parthenophil, a youth whom he has met in Greece. Parthenophil's beauty and eloquence are at once perceived by Thamasta, who falls madly in love. She first has her servant approach the visitor; then she goes to Parthenophil and offers herself to him. The youth politely rejects her advances; and, when she persists, he confides that he is not a man, but a maid, and swears her to secrecy. The disappointed Thamasta promises her silence, even though it soon results in the jealous fury of the unenlightened Menaphon, who now suspects an affair between her and "Parthenophil."

In the meantime, a skilled physician named Corax attempts to cure both Prince Palador and Lord Meleander of their mental illnesses. His methods, though unorthodox, are effective: by presenting a masque with melancholiac characters, Corax tricks the prince into admitting he is a victim of love melancholy and rouses the young ruler from lethargy; by means of a mask and other devices, Corax calms the raving, ax-wielding Meleander and gets the old man to put into words his grief for the missing Eroclea. At this point in the story, "Parthenophil" (who is, of course, Eroclea) completes the therapy begun by the physician. First, she identifies herself to the prince; initially he is incredulous, still thinking her to be Parthenophil, but is convinced when she presents a miniature portrait of him that she has worn in her bosom. Next, she is brought to her father, but only after Meleander has been psychologically prepared for the emotional strain; their reunion is a joyful one. Eroclea then accounts for her strange absence: fleeing from King Agenor, she went to Greece, where for two years she lived disguised as Parthenophil, waiting until she could return to Cyprus with safety. All ends happily for the other characters, too. Menaphon, at one time understandably jealous of "Parthenophil," is reconciled to Thamasta, who has lost her false pride. And Meleander's younger daughter, Cleophila, who has nursed him through his illness, is to marry Thamasta's brother, Amethus.

Although there is no known source for the entire plot of *The Lover's Melancholy,* Ford has done some borrowing (as he himself indicates) from two authors: Famianus Strada (an Italian Jesuit and rhetorician) and Burton. His indebtedness to the former is slight: Menaphon's description of the musical duel between the lute player (Parthenophil) and the nightingale (I.i) is based upon a well-known passage in Strada's *Prolusions,* lines also paraphrased by Richard Crashaw and Ambrose Philips.[2] Ford's indebtedness to Burton is much greater; *The Anatomy of Melancholy* (first published in 1621) exerts an important influence on *The Lover's Melancholy*—and, to a lesser but still significant extent, on at least two of Ford's other plays: *The Broken Heart* and *The Fancies Chaste and Noble.* Burton's book, with its learned yet colorful descriptions of causes, symptoms, and cures, was the best-known study of melancholy in seventeenth-century England, and its approach to personality and neurosis had a wide appeal. In *The Lover's Melancholy,* Ford follows *The Anatomy* closely in Menaphon's description of Palador's symptoms (I.i), in Corax's listing of various forms of physical exercise as effective remedies (II.i), and in Corax's definitions of *Lycanthropia, hydrophobia, dotage, phrenitis, hypochondriacal,* and *Wanton Melancholy* (III.iii).[3] The playwright is also influenced by Burton in a less specific, more pervasive manner, for the topic of his drama is melancholy.

Ford may also have had Shakespeare's *King Lear* in mind when portraying Meleander and Eroclea: their relationship and reunion are like those between Lear and his daughter Cordelia;

and Meleander's comment to Palador, "Great, gracious sir, alas, why do you mock me?/ I am a weak old man" (V.i), is like Lear's when he is regaining his wits: "Pray, do not mock me./ I am a very foolish fond old man" (IV.vii). And *The Queen* (see Chapter 3) could have influenced Ford; if he was its author and if he wrote it before *The Lover's Melancholy*, then the former drama, with its central story of misogyny cured and its subplot of a disdainful lady's contrition, becomes a major source of the latter one.

Ford's use of Burton must not be exaggerated. For one thing, the particular cures effected so successfully in *The Lover's Melancholy* do not come from *The Anatomy*. As the paragraphs to follow show, the recoveries of Palador and Meleander owe much more to Ford's imagination and artistry than to Burton's psychology. Furthermore, though the story of melancholy cured is central, we should not ignore the rest of the play. Eroclea undisguised plays an important role but so does Eroclea disguised; as Parthenophil, she causes not only Thamasta's infatuation (as well as that of the servant Kala) for the "youth" but also Menaphon's jealousy. This pattern of confusion, a type of love triangle already popularized by such plays as Shakespeare's *Twelfth Night* and Beaumont and Fletcher's *Philaster*, is fully developed by Ford; he further expands it by adding an antithetical case of mistaken identity: Grilla, the servant "girl" wooed by the ridiculous courtier Cuculus, is actually a boy in disguise. Thus all parts of *The Lover's Melancholy* are tied together by the same device. Perhaps, as at least one critic has maintained, the work is the weaker for its carefully balanced characters and neatly contrived incidents, but I find in its complexity of arrangement a richness like that of the lute playing so admired by Menaphon:

> there was curiosity and cunning,
> Concord in discord, lines of differing method
> Meeting in one full centre of delight. (I.i)

The phrase "concord in discord" aptly describes the function of Cuculus and Grilla. At first their coarseness, stridency, and grotesqueness seem jarring and extraneous; but, as the play unfolds, their relevance to its "one full centre of delight" becomes clear. Ford's low characters sometimes have been censured for not being funny; perhaps their author had another purpose.

Analysis of Ford's handling of his central story should be preceded by several remarks about his use of *art,* both as word and as concept. The word appears frequently in *The Lover's Melancholy,* first to describe the musical skill of Parthenophil in outdoing the nightingale (I.i) and then, throughout most of the play, to describe the medical skill of Corax, the physician. Concerning the musical duel, commentators have noted little besides Ford's use of Strada, yet the contention between man and bird is not an isolated vignette. Menaphon's narrative repeatedly identifies Parthenophil with art and the nightingale with nature. And, since the bird, unable to match the dexterously played notes of the musician, dies of a broken heart, the entire incident exemplifies art's triumph over nature. As such, the duel parallels and foreshadows Corax's role in the drama. Like the lutist Parthenophil, the physician is associated with *art:* he takes pride in it (II.i); Aretus refers to him as one "singular in art" (III.iii); Sophronos calls him "a perfect arts-man" (III.iii); and Rhetias, though at first a scoffer, soon likens his art to the sun shining "i' th' full meridian of his beauty" (IV.ii). And, like the musician, Corax outdoes nature; he controls by means of his skill the infirmities of Palador and Meleander. Unlike Parthenophil, he brings not death, but health.

The triumph of art over nature, emblematized by the musical bout and illustrated more fully by the learned Corax, is perhaps even more inclusive in *The Lover's Melancholy.* After all, Corax admits that his skill does have a limit: it cannot supply the one remedy desperately needed by both patients, the missing Eroclea. Yet eventually this remedy is provided, and art again triumphs. We might raise the question as to who is the final agent. Is it Eroclea, now not disguised as Parthenophil and playing a lute but presenting herself to prince and to father with flawless tone and timing? Or is it Ford himself, transmuting psychotherapy into drama?

II *Symptoms and Treatment of Illness*

The main plot of *The Lover's Melancholy* consists of six
scenes in which the two melancholy principals, Palador and
Meleander, alternately appear. The first (II.i), third (III.iii),
and fifth (IV.iii) of these scenes are centered on Palador; the
second (II.ii), fourth (IV.ii), and sixth (V.i), on Meleander.
From the very beginning of Ford's portrayal of Palador (II.i),
he creates a mood of lethargy. Soft music is heard, and the prince
enters with a book. Corax tells Palador that he is neglecting the
prescribed physical exercises and that he fears his own infection
"with the sloth/ Of sleep and surfeit." Palador requests those
present to speak freely of him. Sophronos, Aretus, Corax, Pelias,
and Cuculus do so, then withdraw, leaving him with Rhetias.

Palador again asks Rhetias, whom he trusts, to be candid. Rhetias responds by recalling to his prince the misfortunes of the
missing Eroclea; next, for no apparent reason, he tells a newer
and happier tale: "A young lady contracted to a noble gentleman, . . . being hindered by their jarring parents, stole from
her home, and was conveyed like a ship-boy . . . into Corinth
first, afterward to Athens; where . . . she lived, like a youth,
almost two years . . . till, within these three months or less,—
her sweetheart's father dying some year before or more,—she had
notice of it, and with much joy returned home." Eroclea, explains Rhetias, may have met with similar "safety and fate."
What he does not divulge—and what the audience does not
discover until the final scene—is that he has just described precisely the activities of Eroclea. Then Palador commands Rhetias,
"Open my bosom. . . . Unloose the buttons, man." Rhetias, who
obeys, finds a miniature portrait of Eroclea; thereupon, because
other characters enter, the private conversation ends. In this
scene Ford sets up two devices that, upon their convergence
later in the play, are to cure the lethargic prince: one is the
unknown young lady who has fled to, then returned from,
Greece; the other is the miniature in Palador's bosom, the image
close to his heart.

In the next scene (II.ii), Meleander first appears. Whereas
Palador's grief has been quiet and reserved (only to Rhetias
does he reveal his preoccupation with Eroclea), Meleander's
is vociferous and frenzied. Ford has turned up the volume, so

to speak. Meleander's speech is more distracted and disjointed than the prince's; it is also more copious and metaphorical. And, although the mind of the sorrowing father wanders, it nevertheless dwells upon two themes: his daughter and death. These he combines, treats separately, then again combines. Awaking with a deep groan, he laments: "The raven croak'd, and hollow shrieks of owls/ Sung dirges at her funeral." Next he reflects on the wronged Eroclea:

> when winds and storm
> Drive dirt and dust on banks of spotless snow,
> The purest whiteness is no such defence
> Against the sullying foulness of that fury.

When, soon after, Amethus, Menaphon, Parthenophil, and Rhetias enter, Meleander shifts to the topic of universal vanity and death: "Then your last sleeps seize on ye; then the troops/ Of worms crawl round and feast; good cheer, rich fare,/ Dainty, delicious!" He then considers his own death, and asks for a simple funeral:

> Save charge; let me be buried in a nook:
> No guns, no pompous whining.
> . . . .
> It is not comely to be hal'd to th' earth,
> Like high-fed jades upon a tilting-day,
> In antic trappings.

These remarks lead him back to his daughter and her alleged death: "Eroclea was not coffin'd so; she perish'd,/ And no eye dropp'd save mine."

One way of looking at the six scenes depicting Palador and Meleander is to regard them as three pairs. Of these, the first pair (discussed above) introduces the two characters, and the third shows them being cured. But what does the second accomplish? Here Ford in both scenes uses Corax as a link between past and future, and he does so in a similar manner: the physician succeeds in rousing Palador from lethargy to desire and in guiding Meleander from frenzy to coherence; then he concludes both treatments with the surprising admission that his art is inadequate. This admission is no proof, however, that

Ford is portraying Corax as incompetent; rather, the latter merely has performed the function for which the dramatist has created him: Corax sets the stage for the appearance of Eroclea. That he does not know of her presence until later is beside the point; consistency in his motivation is secondary to Ford's major concern: suspenseful and artistic mental therapy.

Before Corax presents the masque for Palador (III.iii), he has briefly explained the nature of melancholy to Sophronos and Aretus (uncle and tutor of the prince, respectively) and has promised that he soon will uncover the cause of the prince's sadness (III.i). The masque itself is a lecture with illustrations: Corax hands Palador a paper that describes the various maladies being enacted; each of the six masquers enters in appropriate costume and speaks as a particular type of melancholiac; and, after each entry, Corax adds a short definition. When all the masquers exit, Palador points to his paper and asks, "What means this empty space?" Corax replies that the space is for love melancholy, which art cannot "personate." Suppose, continues the physician, that Parthenophil were in love with Thamasta; it would be impossible to "limn his passions in such lively colours/ As his own proper sufferance could express." For love melancholy, explains Corax,

> is the tyrant of the heart; . . .
> It runs a headlong course to desperate madness.
> O, were your highness but touch'd home and throughly
> With this—what shall I call it—devil—

Whereupon the prince interrupts: "Hold!/ Let no man henceforth name the word again"; and the scene ends. Ford's skill is once more evident. Taking two popular dramatic conventions, the masque and madness, he utilizes them to rouse Palador from his habitual lethargy; moreover, Ford does so cleverly and climactically: the prince, since he exemplifies love melancholy, becomes, in effect, a seventh participant in the masque. Again, by having Corax arbitrarily select Parthenophil as an instance of love melancholy, Ford makes Palador associate the "youth" with his own grief about Eroclea—an association exploited fully later in the play.

The second scene devoted to Meleander (IV.ii) is in some

ways like the second one devoted to Palador. Corax is, at times, the skilled physician expertly manipulating his patient and, at other times, the inadequately motivated persona carrying out the playwright's purposes rather than his own. As a manipulator of Meleander, Corax is impressive; instead of producing a masque to jar lethargy, he uses a frightful mask and versatile language to calm frenzy. His methods not only are good theater but sound psychology (and not to be found in Burton). Corax also makes his speech blend with Meleander's, echoing in tone and topic the latter's rambling speeches while leading him gradually from maniacal rant to calm coherence. Upon appearing, Meleander, swinging a poleax, roars like a lion; Corax puts on his mask and shouts, "Stay thy paws,/ Courageous beast; else, lo, the Gorgon's skull,/ That shall transform thee." When Meleander shifts to satire, stating that politicians "do wriggle in/ Their heads first, like a fox, to rooms of state," Corax changes to the same key: "Then they fill/ Lordships; steal women's hearts." Meleander, turning next to illnesses and their cures, asserts that the best physician is a hangman; Corax agrees.

At this point, Corax changes his tactics; feigning sorrow, he takes the initiative in the conversation in order to evoke, rather than echo, a deeper note: "'tis a daughter, sir,/ Snatch'd from me in her youth, a handsome girl." This ruse prompts Meleander to put into words the cause of his own despondency: insensibility has afforded an escape from unbearable grief. Now expressing himself with sanity and logic, Meleander berates Corax as a foolish physician unable to cure his own neurosis; Corax docilely agrees. Then, as the scene ends, Corax says in an aside to Meleander's daughter Cleophila, "Have you prepared his cup?" For the first half of this scene, Corax's motivation has been clear enough. But what purpose can he have in making Meleander scoff at his skill, or in having the wine cup "prepared"—especially since Corax still does not know that Eroclea has returned? The answer again seems to be that, in these matters, Corax is not his own man but Ford's.

III   *The Cure*

The Lover's Melancholy has now reached its climax, which is to be a double or two-step one and constitutes the last two scenes (IV.iii and V.i). First comes the cure of Palador. Appearing early in the scene, the prince has lost his sluggishness. Within him, he says, there is "a masculine, a stirring spirit"; Corax has done well. When Palador learns that Parthenophil has disappeared, he brusquely orders those present to find the youth. Alone, he voices his inner turmoil:

> the very soul of reason
> Is troubled in me:—the physician
> Presented a strange masque, the view of it
> Puzzled my understanding; but the boy—

He continues as Rhetias enters: "Parthenophil is lost, and I would see him;/ For he is like to something I remember/ A great while since, a long, long time ago." Rhetias replies that, although Parthenophil has strangely vanished, he has found a "wench" who looks just like him. Both men agree this must be the youth disguised, and Rhetias leaves in order to fetch him. Here we should note how carefully Ford has prepared for the ensuing entry of Eroclea. First of all, she is to appear as herself, that is, "disguised" as a woman. But, second, Palador still believes he has to deal with Parthenophil; the "youth" reminds him of something, but the prince (consciously, at least) has not made the connection. The dramatic function of the earlier, seemingly fortuitous associations contrived by Ford—Rhetias's telling Palador of the young lady who returned home after fleeing in disguise (II.i) and Corax's pointing to Parthenophil as a hypothetical instance of love melancholy (III.iii)—now becomes clear: the prince's recognition of Eroclea has been and is about to be subtly developing and suspenseful rather than instantaneous.

The prince, again alone, expresses his love melancholy in terms of music:

> The music
> Of man's fair composition best accords
> When 'tis in consort, not in single strains:
> My heart has been untun'd these many months,
> Wanting her presence, in whose equal love
> True harmony consisted.

While he is soliloquizing, Eroclea enters behind him and speaks.

And, just as in the preceding scene Corax has blended his speech with Meleander's, so here Eroclea strikes the exact pitch of the prince's mood, to achieve "true harmony":

> Minutes are number'd by the fall of sands,
> As by an hourglass; the span of time
> Doth waste us to our graves, and we look on it:
> An age of pleasures, revell'd out, comes home
> At last, and ends in sorrow; but the life,
> Weary of riot, numbers every sand,
> Wailing in sighs, until the last drop down;
> So to conclude such calamity in rest.

Palador, hearing but not yet seeing this other person, responds: "What echo yields a voice to my complaints?" Eroclea comes forward, kneels before him, and says:

> Let the substance
> As suddenly be hurried from your eyes
> As the vain sound can pass[, sir, from] your ear,
> If no impression of a troth vow'd yours
> Retain a constant memory.

These words could be taken as adequate identification of Eroclea, but Palador sees before him only the youth Parthenophil, whom he now persists in chastising as a heartless impostor. In response to these doubts, Eroclea uses the same tone that marked her first words to him: she describes herself as "worn away with fears and sorrows" and as "wint'red with the tempests of affliction"; she refers to Palador's disbelief as a "burial without pity"; and she asks only "a convoy to [her] grave." Ford thus delays and prolongs Palador's recognition of Eroclea and thereby creates a suspenseful dilemma. The playwright resolves it by means of a device he has planted earlier in the play, the miniature portrait; Palador, we recall, showed Rhetias the "tablet" of Eroclea worn close to his heart (II.i). It is now Eroclea's turn. When Palador says, "If thou beest Eroclea, in my bosom I can find thee," she replies, "As I, Prince Palador, in mine," and she draws forth her miniature of him. This undeniable token of identity Palador immediately accepts, receives "Parthenophil" as Eroclea and his bride-to-be, and casts off melancholy forever.

The final scene of *The Lover's Melancholy* presents the curing of Meleander. Once again Ford's skill is evident, both in the terminating incident and in its relationship to what has preceded. As the scene begins, Corax, speaking to Cleophila, has just learned from her the truth about her sister. Hence the physician, when he earlier "drenched" Meleander's cup with sleeping potion, could not have included Eroclea's reappearance in his intended therapy for her father; as previously, Corax seems to be executing Ford's plans more than his own. Cleophila performs a similar function when, in anticipation of Meleander's meeting Eroclea, she hopes that "with/ Comfort he may, by degrees, digest/ The present blessings in a moderate joy"; for she describes the very sort of experience Ford has in mind for her father. Much later in the scene, when Meleander appears, he is carried in, asleep, on a couch. At the request of Corax, his hair and beard have been trimmed, and he has been dressed in new clothes. Soft music—"Fly hence, shadows, that do peep/ Watchful sorrows charm'd in sleep"—awakens him. Greeted by Corax, Meleander calls him "bear-leech." Corax explains that he already has been given "physic" and is about to receive a "cordial." Meleander, who again berates him, states that "all the hands of art cannot remove/ One grain, to ease my grief." Corax replies, "I'll burn my books, old man,/ But I will do thee good, and quickly too."

In the spectacular cure soon to follow, Ford demonstrates his grasp of human nature: Meleander is too old and too despondent for any sudden revelation about or of his missing daughter. Somehow a more positive attitude must be induced in him gradually, and somehow a smooth transition must then be made from this more receptive mood to the experience of meeting Eroclea. Ford's artistic solution is as impressive as his psychological insight. In quick succession, three characters (Aretus, Amethus, and Sophronos) come to Meleander to explain that they have been sent by Prince Palador of Cyprus to bestow upon Meleander certain honors. Each then gives him an object symbolizing an honor; each announces that the prince will come shortly; and each then departs. First enters Aretus, carrying a patent; it restores Meleander's former privileges and adds the marshalship of Cyprus. Next enters Amethus, with a staff; it represents Meleander's appointment as Grand Commander of the Ports. Then enters Sophronos, with a tablet; it signifies the prince's desire to call Meleander father. After each messenger has left, Corax indicates that these visitations are part of the "cordial" he has promised: "There's one pill works"; "D'ye feel your physic stirring yet?"; "What hope now of your cure?" In its overt repetition, the entire episode is like the earlier masque of melancholiacs (III.iii). Also like the masque, it has helped to mitigate despondency; for Meleander's outlook has brightened considerably. And this improvement has occurred "by degrees": in three steps.

Ford's next accomplishment is to make the shift from Meleander's newly acquired attitude to his orderly acceptance of Eroclea. As his principal device, the dramatist uses, as he did for Palador's cure (IV.iii), a miniature portrait (but this time the likeness is of Eroclea, not of the prince). The "tablet" has a double function: on the one hand, it betokens the third and highest honor conferred by the prince and hence is pleasurable to Meleander; at the same time, its image is that of the missing daughter. Thus Meleander is forced to contemplate Eroclea in a mood that is almost cheerful. Surely he now is psychologically prepared for the reunion. But Ford has in store one additional cushion for the shock of recognition; there is to be not the slightest jar. In earlier scenes, the playwright has depicted rapport between two characters by means of sound: Corax has calmed Meleander by matching the volume and tone of his rants (IV.ii); Eroclea has approached Palador by attuning her speech to the mournful key of his deepest feelings (IV.iii). Now reunion will be achieved by means of sight; almost imperceptibly, shadow will be replaced by substance. Meleander looks at the portrait, and exclaims:

> Eroclea!—'tis the same, the cunning arts-man
> Falter'd not a line. Could he have fashion'd
> A little hollow space here, and blown breath
> T' have made it move and whisper, 't had been excellent:—
> But, faith, 'tis well, 'tis very well as 'tis,
> Passing, most passing well.

There enters a fourth messenger bearing a gift from the prince.

The messenger is Cleophila; the gift is Eroclea. The latter kneels
before her father, and asks, "Dear sir, do you know me?" And
Meleander replies:

> Yes, thou art my daughter,
> My eldest blessing. Know thee! why, Eroclea,
> I never did forget thee in thy absence.
> Poor soul, how dost?

Transition has been executed flawlessly: the recognition has
been painless. In addition, Meleander's peace of mind will last
because, as Cleophila has prayed for, he tastes his joy with
moderation: "My tears, like ruffling winds lock'd up in caves,/
Do bustle for a vent;—on t'other side,/ To fly out into mirth
were not so comely." Thus is Meleander cured, and all is well.

CHAPTER 5

The Decorum of Dying:
The Broken Heart

I *The Story and Its Sources*

ALTHOUGH the order in which Ford's plays were written
or performed is not known, *The Broken Heart*[1] (first printed
in 1633) and *The Lover's Melancholy* have more than enough in
common to warrant sequential treatment. First of all, they are
the only two of Ford's seven extant plays that belonged to the
King's men (the company for which Shakespeare had written),
and were performed by them at the Blackfriars playhouse. The
other five dramas were printed for Christopher Beeston's companies at the Phoenix. This fact, together with the 1628 licensing
date for *The Lover's Melancholy*, has led Bentley to suggest that
Ford wrote first for the King's men, then for Beeston;[2] if so, the
two works are relatively close together in time.

Besides this external evidence, the plays themselves have some
interesting likenesses. In each, for instance, the main story has
a two-part pattern: in *The Lover's Melancholy*, Palador is cured,
then Meleander; in *The Broken Heart*, Penthea dies of grief,
then Calantha. Again, parts of both bear a striking resemblance
in structure: three bearers of sad news who, in a masquelike
sequence, interrupt a dance to speak to Princess Calantha remind us of the bearers of good news who visit Meleander; Ford
handles the two incidents in much the same way. Another type
of similarity, more subtle but probably more significant, is found

in the attitude and language of Penthea, the central persona of
The Broken Heart. Her most poignant speeches express a las-
situde and a weariness with life that recall lines spoken by
Meleander and by Eroclea. One of many parallels must suffice.
Penthea, having lost her mind, is waiting for death:

> There's not a hair
> Sticks on my head but like a leaden plummet
> It sinks me to the grave. I must creep thither;
> The journey is not long. (IV.ii)

Eroclea, speaking to Prince Palador in the tone of his own
melancholy, says:

> Minutes are number'd by the fall of sands,
> As by an hourglass; the span of time
> Doth waste us to our graves. (IV.iii)

Here, quite possibly, is the most important source for *The Broken
Heart.*

Before considering the play more closely, we may find a summary of its story useful. Orgilus tells his father that he is leaving
Sparta (for Athens) because of what has happened to Penthea,
the woman he loves. Though betrothed to Orgilus, she has been
forced by her brother, Ithocles, to marry the older Bassanes.
This marriage, explains Orgilus, has resulted in her misery, not
only because of the broken betrothal, but because Bassanes, who
has proven to be inordinately jealous, keeps his innocent wife
under constant surveillance and fears the rivalry of Orgilus. By
going to Athens, says Orgilus, he will lessen Bassanes's anxiety
and hence make life more bearable for Penthea. Instead of leaving, however, Orgilus remains in Sparta disguised as a scholar
studying under the philosopher Tecnicus. In the palace gardens
he manages to find the unsuspecting Penthea, identifies himself,
and claims her as his own. But Penthea, though admitting that
she still loves him, vows fidelity to her husband and commands
Orgilus never again to speak to her of love.

Meanwhile, Penthea's brother, Ithocles, returns to Sparta from
Messene as a victorious general and receives a hero's welcome
both from King Amyclas and from Princess Calantha, who

crowns him with a garland. Ithocles soon visits his sister and, perceiving Penthea's hopelessness, is remorseful for having ended her betrothal to Orgilus; she bitterly replies that, since she is not married to the man she loves, she finds herself "a faith-breaker" and "a spotted whore." Though most contrite, Ithocles in turn confides to her his love for Princess Calantha; if Penthea wants vengeance, he says, all she need do is report his presumptuous aspiration to the king. Penthea is sympathetic, however, and offers her assistance.

Their conversation is abruptly terminated by her husband, Bassanes, who rushes in to accuse Ithocles of incest. Bassanes, who soon realizes the madness of his charges, begs his wife's forgiveness; but his marital tyranny proves too much for Penthea, who gradually loses her desire to live. In a later scene, she expresses her utter despair to Calantha, to whom she then wills, "in rites of holiest love," Ithocles; and she pleads with the princess on her brother's behalf. Penthea's effort is successful, for subsequently Calantha, though being wooed by Prince Nearchus of Argos, reveals her preference for Ithocles by dropping her ring at his feet; she then requests and receives her father's sanction to marry him. While these events have been occurring, Orgilus has abandoned his disguise as a scholar and returned to the court, where he gives his blessing to the marriage of his sister, Euphranea, to Prophilus, best friend of Ithocles, and is warmly welcomed by the latter.

But Ithocles's expectation of happiness—marriage to Calantha and friendship with Orgilus—is to prove short-lived; vague but ominous are two prophecies of the oracular philosopher Tecnicus: "The lifeless trunk shall wed the broken heart" and "Revenge proves its own executioner." The catalyst of catastrophe is Penthea, who, having lost her mind and spoken distractedly to her brother, her husband, and her beloved, starves herself to death. No sooner has she died than Orgilus, who from the very beginning has held her brother responsible for her plight, exacts vengeance by trapping Ithocles in a mechanical chair and murdering him. Calantha—now Queen of Sparta, her father having died—sentences Orgilus to die. By choosing to bleed himself to death, Orgilus fulfills one prophecy: "Revenge proves its own executioner." Next, Calantha, after calmly arranging for the

disposition of her kingdom, places a wedding ring on the finger
of her "neglected husband," the slain Ithocles, then dies. Thus
comes to pass the second prophecy: "The lifeless trunk shall wed
the broken heart."

For the main story of *The Broken Heart,* no known literary
source exists. Sherman, who has advanced the hypothesis that
Ford was influenced by the love affair of Sir Philip Sidney and
Penelope Devereux, points out that, just as Penelope was forced
to marry Lord Rich in spite of having been promised to Sidney,
so is Penthea forced to give up Orgilus, her true love, for Bassanes. Sherman also notes that Ford must have known of the
affair since his poem *Fame's Memorial* (1606) is dedicated to
Penelope.[3] This parallel between literature and life, while interesting, scarcely covers the entire play (Orgilus, for example,
differs markedly from Sidney). Davril suggests that Ford's theme
could have come from an earlier play, George Wilkins's *The
Miseries of Enforced Marriage* (1607).[4] George Sensabaugh believes that the play's idealization of love (discussed below) is
affected by the Platonic coterie of Queen Henrietta Maria, wife
of Charles I;[5] Davril disagrees, arguing that *The Broken Heart*
was written too early and, also, that Ford's own pamphlet *Honour Triumphant* (1606) had already shown his interest in Platonic love.[6]

S. Blaine Ewing, Jr., contends that the play, like *The Lover's
Melancholy,* is influenced by Burton's *The Anatomy of Melan-
choly* and cites the detailed symptoms of Bassanes's jealousy
(II.i), as well as Ithocles's "passion of ambition" and the melan-
choly of both Penthea and Orgilus.[7] Other commentators have
found other possible origins for various parts of *The Broken
Heart.* Hazlitt thinks that the interrupted dance (V.ii) was suggested by a scene in Marston's *The Malcontent* (1604);[8] William
Gifford finds analogues for Orgilus's mechanical chair in the
Greek topographer Pausanias, the sixteenth-century Italian author
Matteo Bandello, and Barnes;[9] and Davril cites, as a probable
source for Calantha's marriage-in-death to Ithocles, the Spanish
tragedy *Doña Inès de Castro* by La Cerda.[10]

II *Love, Revenge, and Fate*

The theme of *The Broken Heart* is that marriage should be

based upon love. Though not denying the authority of father or brother, Ford emphasizes that enforced marriage has tragic consequences. In the play are three pairs of lovers: Orgilus and Penthea, Ithocles and Calantha, and Prophilus and Euphranea. The third pair are happily wedded, and the lyrics of the song celebrating their nuptials (III.iv) indicate clearly that Ford is not attacking marriage; if not abused, this institution results in the greatest fulfillment of the love between man and woman. But Ithocles has abused it, since he has made his sister break her betrothal to Orgilus; and betrothals are not to be treated so casually.[11] Because of his thoughtlessness, four people die.

Throughout *The Broken Heart* various characters, even minor ones, inveigh against enforced marriage. King Amyclas welcomes Prince Nearchus as a suitor of his daughter but states he will not "enforce affection by our will" (III.iii); and Nearchus later refers to Orgilus and Penthea as "injur'd/ By tyranny or rigor of compulsion" (IV.ii). Of all the characters, Penthea is the most eloquent. Because her betrothal to the man she loves has been violated, she regards her marriage to Bassanes as tainted. To be sure, she will not commit, or even contemplate, adultery; at the same time, she is afflicted by a "divorce betwixt . . . body and . . . heart" (II.iii); with scathing irony, she asks her brother to kill her as "a faith-breaker,/ A spotted whore"; and then she explains: "For she that's wife to Orgilus and lives/ In known adultery with Bassanes/ Is at best a whore" (III.ii). Later, in her madness (IV.ii), she speaks the same language: "There is no peace left for a ravish'd wife/ Widow'd by lawless marriage" (IV.ii).

Love is an important element in *The Broken Heart,* and it is handled in various ways by Ford. He often associates love with beauty, and at times he treats each Platonically. Orgilus, describing the love between himself and Penthea, says that "an interchange/ Of holy and chaste love, so fix'd our souls/ In a firm growth of union, that no time/ Can eat into the pledge" (I.i); and he later calls their relationship "that precious figure/ Seal'd with the lively stamp of equal souls" (II.iii). Ford's Platonic idealization of beauty appears in the first of the play's four songs, which states that anything is less impossible *"than by any praise [to] display/ Beauty's beauty; such a glory/ As beyond all fate, all story"* (III.ii).

be ever, ever dying" (IV.iii). In *Perkin Warbeck,* similar imagery portrays Katherine Gordon, who, like Penthea, suffers nobly in the cause of love.

Love may be the principal element in *The Broken Heart,* but it is not the only one; for revenge and fate are of considerable importance. Ford skillfully uses them to pace his story and to achieve a denouement nicely poised between expectation and surprise. In *The Lover's Melancholy,* we recall, he employs disguise (Eroclea-Parthenophil) as the device to connect his main story of Palador and Meleander to his secondary story of Thamasta and Menaphon; also, he presents a series of six scenes, swinging back and forth between the melancholy prince and the melancholy father in their gradual recoveries. In *The Broken Heart,* no such symmetry of structure is noticeable. Nevertheless, Ford's manipulation of his material is equally impressive, as in his use of revenge.

The avenger is, of course, Orgilus, who murders Ithocles in the last scene of Act IV, immediately after Penthea has died. Ford's timing and emphasis are masterful. Orgilus does not murder Ithocles until Penthea has gone mad and clearly is dying (IV.ii). By thus delaying Orgilus's revenge, Ford gives himself time to develop the love affair between Ithocles and Calantha, who shortly before Penthea's death receive King Amyclas's permission to marry; hence, Orgilus's vengeance is doubly sweet, for he deprives Ithocles not only of life but of the marital bliss Ithocles once took from him. Yet from the very beginning of the play Ford manages, by means of clever emphasis, to present Orgilus as a sinister figure. True, in retrospect and analysis we realize he cannot murder until Penthea dies; but, if we were witnessing the drama for the first time, we could not know this fact. Ford repeatedly reminds us that Orgilus is up to no good—precisely what, we do not know, until the trap is sprung. Orgilus himself keeps us worried: he disguises himself as a scholar, then returns undisguised to the court, where he is arranging some sort of entertainment and where he responds cryptically to Ithocles's proffered friendship. Other characters are suspicious: the philosopher Tecnicus twice warns him (I.iii and III.i), concluding with a lecture that defines and praises honor while damning, among several things, revenge and

murder; his father Crotolon chastises him (III.iv) for the "wolf
of hatred snarling in [his] breast."

As an avenger, Orgilus could be said to represent free will; for
he decides how, where, and when he will consummate the murder; and he strikes like lightning. But if, in *The Broken Heart*,
revenge provides surprise, fate provides expectation, because all
has been foreseen by the gods. Here Ford's principal device is
the ambiguous prophecy made by Tecnicus. When the "inspired"
philosopher utters it to Ithocles and to Orgilus (IV.i), neither
they nor the audience can fathom its import; it must be spelled
out by subsequent events. As Prince Nearchus says, in the play's
last two lines, "The counsels of the gods are never known/ Till
men can call th'effects of them their own" (V.iii). Thus Tecnicus's prophecy to Orgilus that "Revenge proves its own executioner" makes no sense until Orgilus is later bleeding himself to
death for having slain Ithocles. Ford further develops the element of fate by frequent reference to the omniscience of the
gods; as Tecnicus says to Orgilus:

> This change
> Of habit, and disguise in outward view,
> Hides not the secrets of thy soul within thee
> From their quick-piercing eyes, which dive at all times
> Down to thy thoughts. (I.iii)

In this manner Ford adds an air of inevitability to his story without revealing its outcome; *The Broken Heart* offers both expectation and surprise.

III *Decorum and Death*

Also noteworthy in *The Broken Heart* is the decorum, the sense
of propriety, of its characters. Most of them exhibit a restraint
that often complements the thread of fate running through the
play. At times, this decorum amounts simply to the good manners of aristocrats; at other times, it is not only courtly etiquette
but breathtaking Stoicism, for these Spartans die well. In *The
Broken Heart*, the higher one's rank, the more polished his manners: Princess Calantha and Prince Nearchus invariably do and
say the right thing; Ithocles, Orgilus, and Penthea are sometimes

censurers and sometimes the censured; Prophilus twice is socially
remiss; and the soldier-courtiers Groneas and Hemophil are
ludicrously inept. On three occasions Ithocles is politely reprimanded for rudeness by Nearchus, who says of him:

> A gallant man at arms is here, a doctor
> In feats of chivalry, blunt and rough-spoken,
> Vouchsafing not the fustian of civility,
> Which less rash spirits style good manners. (IV.i)

This constant concern, in rather ordinary situations, about proper
behavior may strike some as snobbishness; but Ford is setting
his stage for extraordinary decorum: the deaths of Orgilus and
Calantha. Penthea and Ithocles also die, but they have little
opportunity for mannerliness: Penthea, having lost her mind,
speaks disjointedly and passionately; Ithocles, fatally stabbed,
has time only to voice his courage. Orgilus and Calantha die
with more propriety.

Orgilus, after he has admitted his murder of Ithocles and has
been condemned to die by Calantha, chooses to bleed himself
to death. But, since veins in both arms are to be pierced, he
needs assistance; he requests such aid, politely:

> Only I am a beggar to some charity
> To speed me in this execution,
> By lending th'other prick to th'tother arm
> When this is bubbling life out. (V.ii)

Bassanes readily volunteering, Orgilus thanks him: "Gramercy,
friendship./ Such courtesies are real which flow cheerfully/ Without an expectation of requital." And, even as his blood streams
forth "like a lusty wine new broached," Orgilus remains properly deferential: "On a pair-royal do I wait in death:/ My sov-
ereign, as his liegeman; on my mistress,/ As a devoted servant;
and on Ithocles,/ As if no brave yet no unworthy enemy."

Calantha's death, though not so spectacular, is ultimately more
impressive. At first her reaction to the messengers who announce
the deaths of Amyclas, Penthea, and Ithocles seems mere haugh-
tiness; she refuses to halt the dance, then censures them for
rudeness:

> 'Tis, methinks, a rare presumption
> In any who prefers our lawful pleasures
> Before their own sour censure, t' interrupt
> The custom of this ceremony bluntly. (V.ii)

But empty formalism proves to be supreme Stoicism. For, after she has calmly sentenced Orgilus and arranged for the succession to her throne, Calantha reveals her intolerable suffering:

> O, my lords,
> I but deceiv'd your eyes with antic gesture,
> When one news straight came huddling on another
> Of death, and death, and death. Still I danc'd forward;
> But it struck home, and here, and in an instant. (V.iii)

Her duties having been performed, she kisses Ithocles, orders her dirge sung, and dies of a broken heart.

Bassanes, too, contributes significantly to the play's pattern of decorum, primarily as a foil. Whereas the dominant tone is reserved, hushed, and cadenced, his voice is coarse, raucous, and uneven. In his first appearance, he threatens his servant Phulas:

> I'll tear thy throat out,
> Son of a cat, ill-looking hound's-head, rip up
> Thy ulcerous maw, if I but scent a paper,
> A scroll, but half as big as what can cover
> A wart upon thy nose, a spot, a pimple,
> Directed to my lady. It may prove
> A mystical preparative to lewdness. (II.i)

He sounds the same when next heard (II.iii), berating another hapless servant, Grausis: "Fie on thee! Damn thee, rotten maggot, damn thee!" But his impropriety reaches its nadir when, poniard in hand, he breaks into the private conference between Ithocles and Penthea to call the brother "one that franks his lust/ In swine-security of bestial incest" (III.ii). And Ithocles has just questioned the etiquette of his intrusion, saying "The meaning of this rudeness?" and "I'd say you were unmannerly." Thus Bassanes is Ford's deliberately discordant note, which by its very abnormality reminds us of the harmonious scale of decorum elsewhere.

Later in the play, the dramatist utilizes Bassanes quite differently, making him reinforce rather than clash with the Stoicism of Orgilus's death. Orgilus, soon after he has privately murdered Ithocles, tells Bassanes that he will divulge "an unmatched secret" if Bassanes will "put on . . . such a patience/ As chronicle or history ne'er mentioned." Bassanes replies that nothing Orgilus can say will ruffle his composure:

> be resolute
> The virgin bays shall not withstand the lightning
> With a more careless danger than my constancy
> The full of thy relation; could it move
> Distraction in a senseless marble statue,
> It should find me a rock. (V.i)

Such a metamorphosis of the foul-mouthed and foulminded husband of the earlier scenes actually occurs, for Bassanes lives up to his words; during the subsequent death of Orgilus, nothing can shock him. With alacrity he assists Orgilus, supervising the filleting and pricking of his arms. Armostes, Hemophil, and Groneas are stunned as the fountains of blood jet forth; but Bassanes relishes the experience:

> This pastime
> Appears majestical; some high-tuned poem
> Hereafter shall deliver to posterity
> The writer's glory and his subject's triumph. (V.ii)

Bassanes's enthusiasm seems callous, if not morbid; for Orgilus, not he, is dying. Yet Ford seems more interested in theatrical effect than in characterization: his addition of Bassanes's almost unnerving calm to the awesome steadfastness of Orgilus results in an intensity that is overpowering.

IV   *Structure, Song, and Spectacle*

Ford's dramaturgy calls for additional discussion. Some aspects of it have already been mentioned—his handling of suspense in terms of revenge and fate, his presentation of death in terms of decorum and Stoicism—but we need to examine his use of structure, song, and spectacle. Concerning structure, Ford builds *The*

Broken Heart around two deaths: those of Penthea and Calantha.
One problem he encounters is that of timing. Until Penthea dies,
no one else can: Orgilus has no adequate motivation for murdering Ithocles (not to mention taking his own life); and Calantha,
in turn, has no cause whatsoever for dying of a broken heart.
Yet Penthea dies rather late in the play (IV.iii). One of Ford's
probable reasons (already discussed) is to delay Orgilus's revenge until Ithocles is betrothed to the princess. But another,
and more important reason, should be obvious: Penthea does
not die any sooner because she is Ford's central character. She,
more than any other persona, establishes the prevailing tone of
heartbreak and hopelessness; her lines are the most poignant.
Between her first appearance (II.i) and her death (IV.iii), she
is the major figure in four scenes, three of them private and
extremely personal conversations with Orgilus (II.iii), with
Ithocles (III.ii), and with Calantha (III.v). In her last appearance (IV.ii), having lost her sanity, she addresses husband,
lover, and brother. Her death, coming from a broken spirit and
self-imposed starvation, is slow and deliberate.

But, once Penthea has died, Ford must increase the pace of
his story. He has presented one death in the first four acts; he
now has to present three more in the last four scenes. At the
same time, he must preserve the drama's tone of restraint and
inevitability. Most readers would agree that he succeeds in doing
so. Admittedly, Orgilus's murder of Ithocles is rapid, not slow;
but, since this act is revenge, Ford wishes it to shock. His
handling of the last two deaths re-establishes the mood shattered
briefly by Orgilus; for both Orgilus and Calantha die with de-
liberateness and decorum. Calantha's death may be more unexpected than that of Orgilus, but with her testament and her
dirge in our ears—as well as Tecnicus's prophecy that "the lifeless trunk shall wed the broken heart"—we experience her end
with no great surprise.

The structure of Act I also requires attention. Here Ford carefully sets up a central situation which he then discards in Act II.
In the first act, Orgilus, instead of leaving for Athens, remains
in Sparta disguised as a scholar. In the palace gardens he over-
hears Prophilus wooing his sister, Euphranea (I.iii). When she
responds with a declaration of her love, Orgilus expresses, in

asides, his vexation; for earlier (I.i) he has exacted from Euphranea a promise that she will accept no suitor without his permission. At this point the disguised Orgilus, calling himself Aplotes, greets Prophilus and Euphranea and agrees to Prophilus's suggestion that he carry letters between the two lovers and that he be available for such service twice a day, at nine in the morning and at four in the afternoon. We therefore anticipate an ironic parallel. Just as Ithocles has thwarted the love between his sister Penthea and Orgilus, so will Ithocles obstruct the love between his sister Euphranea and Prophilus (who, in addition, is Ithocles's best friend).

But our expectations are not fulfilled. Letters never are delivered. Orgilus soon abandons his disguise, returns to court, and sanctions his sister's marriage to Prophilus, who after his prominent role in Act I becomes a very minor character. Orgilus eventually destroys a marriage, but it is that of Ithocles and Calantha. As to why Ford dropped his original plan we can only speculate. Perhaps he found the suffering Penthea more interesting to develop than the avenging Orgilus; perhaps he decided that sustaining Orgilus's scholar disguise would be burdensome. At any rate, a major shift in plot occurs after Act I.

Song is also important in *The Broken Heart;* four lyrics, more than in any other work by Ford, not only add a distinct yet harmonious voice to the play but also contribute to its unity. All deal with love; the first might be called philosophical, the second joyful, and the third and fourth mournful. Of the four songs, the first (III.ii) is the most tenuously connected to the story. Praising the ineffable nature of "Beauty's beauty," it is sung while Bassanes awaits outside Ithocles's chamber and Ithocles and Penthea confer within. The Platonic idealism of the lyric seems out of place when succeeded by Bassanes's suspicions of incest:

> The floor is matted,
> The bedposts sure are steel or marble. Soldiers
> Should not affect, methinks, strains so effeminate. . . .
> Chamber-combats
> Are felt, not heard. (III.ii)

But this contrast is intentional; the playwright is utilizing a dramatic device popularized by Fletcher and employed by other

Elizabethan and Stuart dramatists. Many of Fletcher's plays
contain love scenes introduced by erotic lyrics sung offstage; in
Ford's *The Lady's Trial,* such a song begins the incident (II.iv)
in which Adurni, banqueting with Spinella in his chamber, attempts to seduce her. The song in *The Broken Heart* is similar
to these in its context, since man and woman are in a private
chamber, but dissimilar in its lyrics, which are not erotic. Hence
it has a double function: to the inordinately jealous Bassanes,
its context signifies sexual love; to the audience, its chaste words
refute such a suspicion.

Of the play's other songs, the second one is sung, presumably
by Orgilus, to bless the forthcoming marriage of his sister, Euphranea, and Prophilus. As a prothalamum, it prays for "*Com-
forts lasting, loves increasing,/ . . . . Plenty's pleasure, peace
complying*" (III.iv). These lyrics, not to mention the well-
matched couple themselves, should give pause to commentators
who view *The Broken Heart* as simply an attack upon marriage.
The third and fourth songs are dirges, the former for Penthea's
death (IV.ii) and the latter for Calantha's (V.iii); and music
connects thereby the play's two climactic scenes. Calantha dies
much more quickly than Penthea, but Ford creates, by means of
dirge (as well as Calantha's decorum), an effect of equal slow-
ness. In addition, the lyrics for Calantha are associated with
two of Penthea's earlier speeches; the song's first four lines are
quite similar to Penthea's lament to the princess (III.v):

> *Glories, pleasures, pomps, delight, and ease*
> > *Can but please*
> *Th'outward senses when the mind*
> *Is not untroubled or by peace refin'd.*

And the entire dirge, since it is sung by three voices, becomes a
fulfillment of Penthea's pathetic madness: "Sure if we were all
sirens we should sing pitifully,/ And 'twere a comely music when
in parts/ One sung another's knell" (IV.ii).

The Broken Heart was written to be seen as well as heard.
Ford makes effective use of spectacle; gesture, posture, and
grouping assume unusual significance, especially in the portrayal of love and of death. For example, we have the love of

Orgilus and Penthea. When they meet in the grove (II.iii), Penthea clasps his hand, kisses it, and kneels before him; then Orgilus kneels. Later (IV.ii) Penthea, now mad, again clasps his hand and kisses it; then he kisses hers. Such actions make their love seem ceremonial and give it an air of sanctity. Furthermore, the clasping of hands associates the lovers visually with the two happily betrothed couples, who make the same gesture: Euphranea and Prophilus are so united by Orgilus (III.iv) and Calantha and Ithocles by King Amyclas (IV.iii).

Ford also utilizes spectacle for death. A good example is the sedentary pose of Penthea and Ithocles. In their interview (III.ii), brother and sister sit close together; later, Penthea dies in a chair (IV.iii) and is joined in this attitude of death by Ithocles (IV.iv), who is murdered in a chair next to hers. This grouping is paralleled in the final scene, when Calantha is united with Ithocles in death. Ford's stage directions are both detailed and ambiguous: *"Enter four bearing Ithocles on a hearse, or in a chair . . . ; place him on one side of the altar."* Is Ithocles to lie on a hearse, or sit in a chair? And, when Calantha later kisses him, then dies, what is her posture of death? We wish that Ford had left no choice other than the sedentary posture; but, even without it, the concluding tableau would bring to mind the earlier one.

Finally, something should be said about the language of *The Broken Heart*, particularly its depiction of character and its linking of scenes. To portray character, Ford in some cases employs throughout the drama similar imagery, the cumulative effect of which is considerable. Ithocles, for instance, time and again is described in terms of rising and falling—the rise is usually presumptuous, and the fall is usually precipitous. Soliloquizing, he likens his ambition to a blinded dove that mounts to clouds only to tumble "headlong down" (II.ii) and to fireworks that "fly into the air" only to "vanish/ In stench and smoke" (II.ii). Armostes compares Ithocles to Ixion, who, "aiming/ To embrace Juno, bosom'd but a cloud/ And begat centaurs" (IV.i); Orgilus compares him to Phaeton (IV.iv), who drove the sun chariot until blasted from the heavens by Zeus; and Nearchus likens him to "low mushrooms" (IV.i) and refers to him as "lord ascendant" (IV.ii). Together, all these images clearly picture Ithocles as an upstart and prefigure his sudden downfall. Ford portrays Bassanes in a similar manner; for animal imagery repeatedly connotes the bestial, degrading attitudes of the jealous husband.

Ford also uses language to link scenes (the similar function of song and of spectacle has been noted above), establishing connections where, logically, none should exist. Two examples may be given. King Amyclas, joyfully anticipating the return of the victorious general Ithocles, says: "I shall shake off/ This silver badge of age, and change this snow/ For hairs as gay as are Apollo's locks" (I.ii). In the first scene of Act II, when Bassanes asks his servant Phulas for news, the latter replies:

> Forsooth, they say the king has mew'd
> All his gray beard, instead of which is budded
> Another of pure carnation color,
> Speckled with green and russet.

As characterization, Phulas's speech is worthless; but its repetition of hair imagery reminds the audience of the king's earlier comment about Ithocles. Another illustration involves Ford's two principal death scenes. Orgilus, as he leaves the dead Penthea and Ithocles, addresses them: "Sweet twins, shine stars forever" (IV.iv); King Amyclas, in the preceding scene (IV.iii), has employed the same epithet for Calantha and Ithocles: "Sweet twins of my life's solace." Once more Ford makes an association solely by repeated words. And this connection is an important one, for if, before the final death (V.iii), the audience has already associated the two couples verbally, it cannot fail to associate them visually when Calantha joins Ithocles in death.

CHAPTER 6

"Impostor beyond Precedent":
Perkin Warbeck

I *The Story and Its Sources*

THE next play to be considered is *The Chronicle History of Perkin Warbeck*,[1] first published in 1634. No external evidence associates it with the two dramas already discussed; both *The Lover's Melancholy* and *The Broken Heart* belonged to the King's men, while *Perkin Warbeck* and Ford's other major plays were written for Beeston's companies. Yet *Perkin Warbeck*, Ford's only history play, recalls *The Broken Heart* in several ways: Warbeck's "resolution" throughout the drama seems an expansion of Ithocles's Stoical acceptance of death; Katherine Gordon's enforced marriage to Warbeck, at least in the earlier acts, appears to be based upon the unhappy lot of Penthea; and there are many verbal parallels.

As the play begins, we find King Henry VII with his counselors at Westminster. While thankful that the late civil wars are ended, he resents the "fresh coals of division" fanned by Margaret of Burgundy in her protégé, Perkin Warbeck, who claims the English throne. Elsewhere, Warbeck, arriving at the court of King James of Scotland, identifies himself as Richard, Duke of York, son of Edward IV and the rightful king of England. His eloquence and regal bearing so impress the Scottish monarch that he accepts him as "Duke Richard" and promises military support against Henry. James also arranges the marriage of Warbeck to a kinswoman, Lady Katherine Gordon; thereby, James overrides the protests of both her father (the Earl of Huntley) and her suitor (Lord Daliell).

In England, meanwhile, King Henry is beset by several grave problems; but he handles them with skill. One of his aides, Sir Robert Clifford, confesses his treasonous connection with Warbeck and also implicates Henry's lord chamberlain, Sir William Stanley, who soon admits his guilt. The king, although tempted to forgive Stanley, a close friend, realizes he must not; and Stanley is executed. A different sort of threat is posed by his Cornish subjects, who, resenting Henry's levies, march toward London; they are routed at Blackheath by the forces of the king, who punishes the leaders but forgives their misguided followers. As for the double menace of James and Warbeck, Henry's preventive measures are military and diplomatic: anticipating incursions, he sends troops to the border; aiming for a peace treaty with James, he confers with Hialas, an emissary from King Ferdinand of Spain.

Warbeck, his marriage having been royally celebrated at the Scottish court, bids a loving farewell to Katherine as he leaves with James for the wars; in her reply, she assures him of her complete devotion and loyalty. The border raid takes place but is unsuccessful, for Englishmen do not flock round the banner of the "Duke of York"; and, from the walls of the besieged Castle of Norham, Henry's chief adviser, the Bishop of Durham, lectures James on the folly of supporting Warbeck. James eventually withdraws his troops. Shortly thereafter, when he is visited by Durham and the Spaniard Hialas, who urge him to secure peace by marrying Princess Margaret of England and by banishing Warbeck, he accepts their advice.

Taking James's dismissal with resolution, Perkin, accompanied by his wife and counselors, leaves Scotland for Cornwall, where his forces besiege Exeter but are soon defeated. He flees to sanctuary, then gives himself up. Brought before Henry, he remains defiant and is sent to London for imprisonment in the Tower of London. An attempted escape is unsuccessful, and he is put in the stocks. There he is visited by Lambert Simnel, a confessed pretender to the throne, who urges him to admit imposture; Warbeck rejects him with disdain. Another visitor is the ever-faithful Katherine, who, though also captured by Henry's forces, has been treated graciously by the monarch; husband and wife vow their eternal love. Then Perkin, eloquent to the end and described by Henry's aide Dawbeney as an "imposter beyond precedent," is led off to be executed.

In depicting this episode in English history, Ford makes considerable use of two prose sources: Bacon's *History of the Reign of King Henry VII* (1621) and Thomas Gainsford's *True and Wonderful History of Perkin Warbeck* (1618). Many lines in *Perkin Warbeck* are quite similar to passages in one or the other of these chronicles.[2] In this respect, Ford borrows from the two works about equally: more from Bacon in Acts II and V, more from Gainsford in Acts III and IV, and about the same from both in Act I. In his general emphasis, the playwright more closely follows Bacon, whose grasp of personality and politics is much superior to Gainsford's. Ford is, however, by no means fettered by his sources; he adds to, omits from, and alters their accounts very skillfully, rearranging historical sequence and reshaping historical personages—especially his two antagonists, Warbeck and Henry VII. Another, though less direct, influence comes from Shakespeare, whose chronicle plays must have been familiar to Ford. Indeed, *Richard II* probably contains the source (III.ii) for a scene in *Perkin Warbeck*, the pretender's landing in Cornwall (IV.v).[3] Also, Ford's play may be said to continue the earlier dramatist's history of England: in 1485, Henry of Richmond became Henry VII by defeating Richard III at the battle of Bosworth Field, an event depicted in the final act of Shakespeare's *Richard III*.

Why did Ford write *Perkin Warbeck*? More particularly, is it in any way propaganda? History plays often raise such questions, and *Perkin Warbeck* has been no exception. Some twentieth-century critics have viewed it as an attack upon the theory of the divine right of kings, basing their interpretation on Ford's contrast between the far-sighted, realistic policies of Henry VII and the autocratic, impractical attitudes of both Warbeck and James IV.[4] But surely this interpretation is to misread the play with hindsight, making it indict Stuart absolutism in order to anticipate the forthcoming civil war. Although *Perkin Warbeck* by implication criticizes excessive dependence upon divine right,

Henry (who must be regarded as Ford's spokesman) several times supports it. Not only does he believe his throne guarded by "angels" (I.i), but he sees as sacrilegious the rebelling Cornish, whose "disobedience, like the sons o'th' earth,/ Throw a defiance 'gainst the face of heaven" (III.i). More than once Henry stresses not the duties but the privileges of sovereignty. Surrey speaks for him when he says, "In affairs/ Of princes, subjects cannot traffic rights/ Inherent to the crown" (IV.i). Henry also supports the rights of sovereignty when he calls his taxes "voluntary favors as our people/ In duty aid us with" (IV.iv) and when he states that the Cornish, by rebelling, "Deny us what is ours, nay, spurn their lives,/ Of which they are but owners by our gift" (IV.iv). Thus *Perkin Warbeck* does not condemn divine right; instead, Ford accepts the theory while indicating that it should be implemented with intelligence.

Nor, if the play alludes at all to contemporary politics, does the characterization of Warbeck seem intended as an attack upon any individual; Perkin is portrayed too sympathetically. As proof, we need cite only the 1745 revision, which unquestionably identifies Warbeck as the Stuart Pretender, Charles Edward; in the revision, the redeeming love between Warbeck and Katherine is virtually eliminated lest he be too attractive an impostor.[5] Two other possible motives of the playwright should be mentioned. One is that the drama argues against military and financial aid to Frederick, Elector Palatine, who was a brother-in-law of Charles I. Massinger, in *Believe as You List*, a play licensed in 1631, may very well be supporting Frederick; *Perkin Warbeck* could be counterpropaganda. Another possibility is that Ford, by means of his idealized portrayal of Henry VII as a peacemaker, seeks to praise James I. The two monarchs, founders of the Tudor and Stuart dynasties, respectively, were often coupled as lovers of peace and as uniters of kingdoms.[6] Also, Henry had initiated James's eventual succession (1603) by marrying Princess Margaret of England to an earlier King James; Ford includes in his play the arrangements for this match. Furthermore, Ford's own pamphlet *A Line of Life* (1620) praises James I as a peacemaker. If Ford's Henry VII does represent James, then *Perkin Warbeck* probably was written between 1621 (the publication date of Bacon's history) and 1625 (the year of

James's death). These hypotheses must remain conjectural, however, for lack of adequate evidence.

Still another explanation is that Ford, already influenced by Burtonian psychology in *The Lover's Melancholy* and in *The Broken Heart*, sees another instance of it in Warbeck's self-delusion.[7] To the extent that Warbeck sincerely believes himself to be "Duke Richard" and is not just a sly rascal, this idea is valid. Yet we should not view Warbeck simply as a madman possessed with illusions of royalty. Urswick, one of Henry's aides, makes this very diagnosis; but it comes in the final act, long after Warbeck has made his full impact upon the audience. When Perkin is expressing courage, love, or defiance, he is no counterfeit; we forget, temporarily, his imposture.

II   *The Enhancement of Warbeck*

There are other, more plausible reasons for Ford's writing the drama. First, the story of Warbeck, always a fascinating one, had recently been given unusual prominence by the accounts of Bacon and Gainsford; there may also have been an earlier play.[8] Second, Ford saw in the career of Warbeck a potentially effective vehicle for presenting what had been the topic of his pamphlet *The Golden Mean* and an important element in *The Broken Heart*: Stoicism. *Potentially* is an important word because, prior to Ford's play, Warbeck had invariably been portrayed as contemptible, as lacking even the sincerity of a psychopath; and all the chronicles stated that he ultimately read a public confession of his imposture. Clearly Ford has ennobled the traditional Warbeck. In the drama Perkin's lofty language and aspirations may seem presumptuous when he first appears, as a claimant at the court of James (II.i); but they become more and more impressive as he suffers banishment, then imprisonment, then death.

Much of this increase in Warbeck's stature can be explained in terms of *The Golden Mean*, for the play and the pamphlet have interesting similarities. For instance, the greater part of the essay explains, in order, how the truly virtuous man will persevere in spite of "*Disfauour, Neglect,* forfeite of *Estate, Banishment, Imprisonment,* or *Death*"; in the play, Warbeck resolutely undergoes such misfortunes. Again, the entire conversation be-

tween the defiant Warbeck and the confessed pretender Simnel
(V.iii.22–76)—a confrontation invented by Ford—amounts to an
illustration of the following precept in *The Golden Mean:*

> For it is as merely impossible for a great and excellent spirit to conceiue
> thoughts tending to baseness, as for the base to apprehend the singular
> designes belonging to the Noble minded. Soone then it is to be obserued,
> that the distinction betweene a worthy and a seruile person, must be rather
> found out in the qualitie of their mindes, then the command of authority
> and complement. . . . The seruile weaknes of such, whose education, nature,
> experience, and wisedome cannot claime any prioritie in desert, is so great,
> as it onely shewes that it distasteth not calamitie, so long as it is full fed
> with the happinesse of plenty and ease. (9–10)

The play's kinship to *The Broken Heart* also is apparent. Penthea, Ithocles, Orgilus, and Calantha all suffer nobly. So does
Warbeck, and his Stoicism is augmented by that of his wife, her
ill-starred suitor Daliell, and her servant Jane. *Trial, sufferance,*
and *constancy* are often-heard words in *Perkin Warbeck.*

Another likely reason for Ford's dramatizing the Warbeck
episode is his interest in kingship,[9] especially the privileges and
responsibilities of sovereignty. The play's threefold pattern of
kingship—the differing capabilities of Henry, Warbeck, and
James—are discussed later in this chapter. To be noted at this
point is the manifestation of the same interest in three of Ford's
other works: the prose pamphlet *A Line of Life, The Lover's
Melancholy,* and *The Broken Heart.* The first of these shows a
familiarity with political theory, and it concludes with a discussion of the ideal king that bears noteworthy similarities to
Perkin Warbeck. The essay reveals Ford's acquaintance with
Greek and Roman philosophers; it also cites the *Basilicon Doron*
of James I, a work concerned with the proper conduct of a ruler.
In a section on the "public man," Ford, though criticizing the
Dutch leader Barnevelt for excessive "private ambition," ad-
mires him for a political sagacity much like that Ford later portrays in Henry VII: "He was the only one that trafficked in the
counsels of foreign princes, had factors in all courts, intelli-
gencers amongst all Christian nations; . . . , and was even the
moderator of policies of all sorts; was reputed to be second to
none on earth for soundness of designs" (406).

But most relevant to the play is the essay's last section, concerning "a good man." Into this category Ford places kings, for

as one king traffics with another, another, and another, either for repressing of hostilities, enlarging a confederacy, confirming an amity, settling a peace, supplanting an heresy, and suchlike, not immediately concerning his own particular, or his people's, but for moderating the differences between other princes; in this respect even kings are private men, and so their actions belong wholly and only to themselves, printing the royalty of their goodness in an immortality of a vertuous and everlasting name. (413–14)

Hence Ford's ideal king is a statesman, a promoter of peace; and, as his one example, he cites James I: "a good man that, even with his entrance to the crown, did not more bring peace to all Christian nations, yea, almost to all nations of the western world, than since the whole course of his glorious reign hath preserved peace amongst them" (414). Another, later, example is Henry VII in *Perkin Warbeck.*

Ford's interest in kingship also appears in *The Lover's Melancholy* and *The Broken Heart,* though to a lesser extent than in either *A Line of Life* or *Perkin Warbeck.* In *The Lover's Melancholy,* Prince Palador's advisers—Corax, Sophronos, and Aretus—warn him that his melancholy idleness is endangering the kingdom (II.i). Thereupon Palador commands the counselors and courtiers present to speak candidly of his conduct. Sophronos, Aretus, and Corax criticize their monarch; Pelias and Cuculus servilely flatter him; and Rhetias warns that "Princes who forget their sovereignty, and yield to affected passion, are weary of command." This scene anticipates Ford's fuller treatment of the ruler's use of counsel in *Perkin Warbeck.* In *The Broken Heart,* sovereignty twice is alluded to by Orgilus: once, when he mentions subjects' "meek obedience" to their king (III.iv); again, when he states that royalty is derived ultimately from merit, not from birth (IV.iii). Huntley and Daliell raise the same questions in *Perkin Warbeck.*

As for Ford's characterization of Warbeck, it must have been surprising and suspenseful to his audience, who knew only the traditional, despicable Perkin. His first appearance (II.i), where his eloquence charms King James, probably did not contradict any preconceptions of mediocrity and eventual ignominy; but

his ensuing fortitude—especially his refusal to read a confession—
must have seemed a novel depiction of a heretofore infamous
figure. Ford had to be careful, however; he could not suggest
that Warbeck was in truth the son of Edward IV; if he did, he
would, of course, be denying the legitimacy of the Tudor and
Stuart monarchies. His solution is to present Warbeck simultaneously as a noble Stoic and false claimant; the protagonist is
to be admired for his personal relationships but condemned for
his politics. That Ford can make an effective drama of this apparent dilemma testifies to his skill as a playwright.

To enhance Warbeck, Ford utilizes more than Stoicism. Perkin, for example, is utterly sincere in his claim of royalty; even
when, in a private conference, his chief adviser, Frion, implies
an imposture, he is outraged (IV.ii). Ford, understandably, gives
Warbeck no soliloquies; these would only remind the audience
of what the author wants them to forget: the question of Warbeck's sanity. Again, Perkin must be admirable simply because
two of the play's most impressive characters, Katherine and
Huntley, think he is; this psychological device Shakespeare
often employs. Finally, Warbeck's own words ring true, whether
expressing love, defiance, scorn, or courage. We hear him berate
Lambert Simnel, who has urged that he confess imposture and
seek pardon from Henry:

> For pardon? Hold, my heartstrings, whiles contempt
> Of injuries in scorn may bid defiance
> To this base man's foul language.—Thou poor vermin,
> How dar'st thou creep so near me? Thou an earl?
> Why, thou enjoy'st as much of happiness
> As all the swinge of slight ambition flew at.
> A dunghill was thy cradle. So a puddle
> By virtue of the sunbeams breathes a vapor
> To infect the purer air, which drops again
> Into the muddy womb that first exhal'd it. (V.iii)

While Ford thus heightens Warbeck's personal dignity, he also
manages to belittle his political significance. This purpose is
accomplished in various ways. One is to make the scenes with
Henry VII contain those with Warbeck: the play begins at the
court of Henry, who with his aides repeatedly refers to Perkin

as an impostor; the opening and closing lines of the drama are spoken by Henry, who likens himself to a physician who has cured the "rent face/ And bleeding wounds of England's slaughter'd people" (I.i) and who, by executing Warbeck, has restored his country to good health "purged of corrupted blood" (V. iii). Another device is to remind the audience throughout the drama of Warbeck's imposture; Ford fires a steady barrage of uncomplimentary epithets. Still another is to keep the personable Warbeck offstage until Act II, by which time the audience has been permanently convinced that he is a counterfeit. Ford stacks the deck still further; not only all the English characters but most of the Scottish ones, including Katherine, are skeptical of Perkin's claims. Also serving Ford's purpose is Warbeck's quartet of inept counselors—the Mayor of Cork, Heron, Sketon, and Astley—who usually confer not with Perkin but with his chief adviser, Frion; their ludicrous words and actions diminish their leader's political stature without contaminating his dignity as an individual.

III   *The Enhancement of Henry VII*

But Ford's most effective device for containing Warbeck is his characterization of Henry VII. For, if the dramatist has enhanced Warbeck as a Stoic, he has also enhanced the English king as a statesman. The play's Henry is a master of statecraft; he anticipates every move of Warbeck, not to mention James IV. Ford is more favorable to Henry than were any of the chroniclers, who were sympathetic but qualified their praise. Bacon, for example, thinks that Henry lacked foresight and, hence, though a brilliant tactician, was a poor strategist; and he also sees avarice in the king's collecting of subsidies.[10] Gainsford notes confusion in his handling of the Cornish uprising.[11] In *Perkin Warbeck,* the king is flawless; indeed, Ford alters history to increase Henry's wisdom. For instance, the playwright places before, instead of after, the first Scottish incursion Henry's meeting with Hialas (the Spanish emissary) in which a peace treaty between England and Scotland is planned; consequently, when in the following scene (III.iv) James and Warbeck lead in their invading troops, their efforts seem futile and short-sighted. Another example occurs in the fourth scene of Act IV when Henry, anticipating Warbeck's attack on Exeter even before the latter has landed in Cornwall, sends his forces to Salisbury (midway between Exeter and London). In the histories of Bacon and Gainsford, Henry shows no foresight concerning Exeter; and, when it is besieged, his troops are near London, not in Salisbury.

In his idealization of Henry, Ford not only increases foresight but reduces cunning. Unlike some of the chroniclers, the playwright attributes no trickery to the king either in his move to the Tower immediately before Stanley's confession (I.i) or in the Cornish rebels' expecting battle on Monday instead of on Saturday (III.i). Ford's procedure here probably is accounted for by the popularity in contemporary English drama of the "Machiavel" character (a gross distortion of the real Machiavelli), which added atheism and brutality to the more appropriate traits of cunning, dissimulation, and hardheadedness. Ford had to take care that his audience did not mistake Henry for a villain; and, in this respect, his omission of *politic* from the play is noteworthy. The word had been used by historians, such as Edward Hall and Raphael Holinshed, to praise Henry's wisdom; but it became debased on the stage by association with the scheming Machiavel, or "politician."

At the same time, Ford emphasizes Henry's pragmatism: the king often stresses the importance of money, believing that it increases loyalty and manpower; he expertly utilizes his advisers (in contrast to James and Warbeck) and once defers to their counsel; he skillfully delegates authority to his subordinates; he ably metes out justice, whether mercy or punishment. For this concept of the ideal ruler, the playwright probably is influenced by the many treatises *de regimine principum* ("the conduct of princes"), especially those of the more realistic theorists such as Machiavelli and Bacon.

In Ford's depiction of kingship, Warbeck and James are contrasted to Henry. Although the play should not be read as an attack upon the theory of divine right, it does support the *de facto* basis of sovereignty. Henry, while he may be God's appointed deputy, makes sure that his troops are well armed and well paid. Warbeck, on the contrary, depends completely on the *de jure* basis of sovereignty, maintaining that his birthright entitles him to the throne. This argument at first impresses James and induces him to support Warbeck; but, after several expensive raids into English territory have led to no rebellion and after Henry has offered an attractive truce, James adopts the latter's pragmatism and dismisses Warbeck. Warbeck fails politically not because he is a counterfeit but because he is impractical and is encountering a much more competent adversary. When he lands in Cornwall, he calls upon "horrors," "fear," and "numbness" to strike Henry's forces, and he depends greatly on his "divinity of royal birth." Henry relies on the more tangible assets of money, manpower, and treaty; and the outcome of the conflict is never in doubt.

It should be noted that Ford, in his treatment of the Warbeck story, makes a confession by Perkin unnecessary. As previously explained, by the time Warbeck first appears (II.i), Henry and his counselors already have thoroughly described his imposture; in addition, because Ford, as the play progresses, resolves the conflict between Warbeck and Henry in terms of political skill rather than hereditary right, the matter of Warbeck's identity never reappears to demand further consideration. Whether he is a blue-blooded Plantagenet or a compulsive liar is not the question; he dies because Henry time and again has outmaneuvered him. Hence there is no dramatic necessity for a final public confession by Warbeck, and Ford is free to present him as an individual who is invariably eloquent, courageous, and sincere, although disastrously impractical.

Also significant in the play's depiction of kingship is Ford's portrayal of James IV of Scotland, who gradually changes from an irresponsible leader like Warbeck to a realist like Henry. Once again Ford differs from the histories, none of which present the overbearing monarch of the first three acts. In his first speech (II.i), James regards as obligatory the aiding of fallen princes. Impressed by Warback's eloquence and bearing, he offers his support. And he reprimands the skeptical Huntley: "Kings are counterfeits/ In your repute, grave oracle, not presently/ Set on their thrones, with scepters in their fists" (II.iii).

Ford then converts his intractable autocrat into a practical and responsible monarch. He begins the transformation in the last scene of Act III, when he presents the two opposing con-

cepts of kingship that he has carefully kept apart in England
and in Scotland until both have been fully presented. Besieging
Norham Castle with Warbeck, James is confronted by Henry's
ablest subordinate, the Bishop of Durham. Durham, besides
calling Warbeck an impostor, points out to James such con-
siderations as a treaty with Henry, Warbeck's lack of support
in England, and James's duties to his own subjects. James
pauses, "serious,/ Deep in his meditations," while Durham and
Warbeck exhort him, respectively, to peace and to war. After
deliberation, James decides to continue the incursion, but Durham's words have had their effect. For, when Warbeck laments
the suffering that must ensue, the king reprimands him for
foolishness:

> You fool your piety
> Ridiculously, careful of an interest
> Another man possesseth. Where's your faction?
> Shrewdly the bishop guess'd of your adherents
> When not a petty burgess of some town,
> No, not a villager hath yet appear'd
> In your assistance. That should make 'ee whine,
> And not your country's sufferance, as you term it. (III.iv)

And when Frion enters with the news that Surrey has arrived
with twenty thousand men to raise the siege, James immediately
orders a retreat. Thereafter in the play James, with one exception, is conspicuously practical. He does rashly challenge Surrey
to single combat but is offstage when his proposal is declined
by Surrey and Durham in a scene (IV.i) that serves chiefly to
illustrate Henry's skillful delegation of authority. The Scottish
king speaks the language of a realist (and of Henry) when
he accepts the peace offers of Durham and Hialas (IV.ii) and
when, in his last lines, he dismisses Warbeck (IV.iii).

Thus Ford's presentation of kingship in *Perkin Warbeck* is
threefold: between the flawless Henry and the inept Warbeck
is James, who changes from a high-handed ruler to one who
has discovered and adopted, thanks to Henry's examples, a
more practical philosophy. This function of James is underlined
by the final reference to him, when Henry asks Surrey why,
in negotiating the treaty with James, he did not demand restitu-
tion for the border raids:

SURREY.   Both demanded
        And urg'd, my lord, to which the king replied
        In modest merriment, but smiling earnest,
        How that our master Henry was much abler
        To bear the detriments than he repay them.

HENRY.
        The young man, I believe, spake honest truth;
        'A studies to be wise betimes. (V.ii)

While Ford thus creates an arresting pattern of kingship
by manipulating his sources, he increases the pathos of the story
by greatly expanding what is scarcely discernible in the histories:
the roles of Daliell, Huntley, and Katherine. The three Scottish
characters express in terms of individual heartbreak and courage
the consequences of Warbeck's political disaster; they also help
to make him not only credible but admirable. Daliell is entirely
Ford's invention; but, if we want a source for his ill-fated
courtship of Katherine, we need look no further than Orgilus's
plight in *The Broken Heart*. Unlike Orgilus, however, Daliell
harbors no vengefulness when he accompanies Warbeck and
Katherine in their banishment from Scotland; instead, he displays
a selfless courage that, in effect, heightens that of the other two.
As for Huntley, he is largely Ford's creation, for the chronicles
state only that he is Katherine's father. The elderly lord is a
very important character. His words add warmth and wit to
the play; of all the Scots, he alone protests strongly to King
James about Warbeck, speaking not only as an honest counselor
but also as a loving father.

Concerning Katherine, the sources provide a little information;
Bacon states that "in all fortunes she entirely loved [Warbeck];
adding the virtues of a wife to the virtues of her sex."[12] Gainsford presents a lengthy and awkward account of Warbeck's
wooing of Katherine; the two converse in stilted, euphuistic
language.[13] Ford makes no use of Gainsford, unless it be for
Daliell's somewhat affected speech in his courtship of Katherine
(I.ii). Ford's enhancing of Katherine's fidelity to Warbeck may
be partially accounted for by another work, William Warner's
Albion's England (1596), which extols her "great Constancie"
after her husband's death.[14]

On the other hand, Ford may have known, as we now know,
that Katherine in fact married three more times. At any rate,

in *Perkin Warbeck* she is an exemplary wife; and, if Henry diminishes her husband as a political figure, she redeems him not only as a resolute Stoic but as a man capable of loving a woman. At the same time, Ford takes care that the excellence of Perkin's conjugal love never becomes an argument for his political claims; for Katherine herself remains dubious about them. Her doubts begin even before they meet—"I should pity him/ If 'a should prove another than he seems" (II.i)—and reappear shortly after their marriage when, upon Warbeck's casual use of *counterfeit,* she ominously remarks, "Pray do not use/ That word, it carries fate in't" (III.ii). And, when she sees him for the last time in the stocks, she says, "Be what these people term thee, I am certain/ Thou art my husband" (V.iii).

Looking at the structure of *Perkin Warbeck,* we find in the first half a striking pattern of alternation. In *The Lover's Melancholy,* it may be recalled, Ford handles in this manner the six scenes devoted to the curing of Prince Palador and Lord Meleander. In *Perkin Warbeck* the device of alternation is even more pronounced, containing the first nine of the play's eighteen scenes. More specifically, the first, third, fifth, seventh, and ninth scenes are set in England and dominated by Henry VII; the second, fourth, sixth, and eighth scenes take place in Scotland and—with the exception of the second, which presents Katherine, Daliell, and Huntley—are centered on Warbeck and James IV.

The advantages of this structural pattern are many. First of all, it enables Ford to accentuate the contrast in kingship that has already been discussed. For example, two consecutive scenes (II.ii and II.iii) show the use of counsel by Henry and by James: the former defers to Durham's insistent advice that the traitor Sir William Stanley be denied mercy, while the latter overrides the objections of Daliell, Crawford, and Huntley concerning Warbeck. Another advantage is that Ford can present his idealization of Henry cumulatively and thus more forcefully. That is, in the first scene Henry describes Perkin's imposture, in the third he hears Clifford's confession, in the fifth he sentences Stanley, in the seventh he routs the Cornish rebels, and in the ninth he confers with Hialas about a treaty with Scotland. Consequently, by the time James and Warbeck invade England (the tenth scene), the audience can have no doubts as to either Henry's superior wisdom or the eventual failure of the incursion. And Ford is pushing in the same direction in the scenes in Scotland: Warbeck and James do not appear until the fourth scene, by which time Henry has had two scenes in which to impress the audience; furthermore, in the fourth, sixth, and eighth scenes, the imperiousness of James and the impracticality of Warbeck are fully displayed.

In the second half of the play, Ford does not use alternation, principally, no doubt, because the opposing forces have now met. But, if Henry appears in only one (IV. iv) of the five scenes in Act IV, he is ably represented in two of the others (IV.i and IV.iii) by Surrey and Durham; besides, Ford in the earlier scenes has made it clear that Henry has won before the fighting begins. The structure of the later scenes, though not so symmetrical, is nevertheless noteworthy, especially Ford's handling of Warbeck. Because, by the middle of the play, the audience has been convinced that Perkin is an impostor and that he surely will lose, Ford is free to ennoble his protagonist. He does so primarily by presenting him in three meetings, none of them to be found in the sources. The captured Warbeck speaks with King Henry (V.ii), then with the erstwhile pretender Simnel (V.iii), and then with Katherine (V.iii). Ford, by putting the meeting with Henry before the other two, in effect terminates the political conflict early enough for Perkin to dominate the last scene; and Warbeck's contempt for Simnel and love for Katherine, as well as his courageous acceptance of death, are most impressive.

There are no villains in *Perkin Warbeck*. As the play progresses, both Warbeck and Henry grow stronger and more admirable; because their excellences differ in kind—Stoicism for the one, statecraft for the other—the two antagonists complement rather than neutralize one another. Both men triumph: the statesman over his less far-sighted and "provident" adversary; the Stoic, over death.[15]

CHAPTER 7

A Sister's Heart: 'Tis Pity She's a Whore

I The Story and Its Sources

'*T* IS *Pity She's a Whore*[1] (first published in 1633) has been considered by many to be Ford's outstanding work. Certainly, with its story of incest, it has been the most controversial. Some, who have thought it to be the first written of Ford's seven principal plays, base their hypothesis largely upon the phrase "these first fruits of my leisure" in its dedicatory epistle to the Earl of Peterborough. Yet these words may mean only that the drama was the first product of a particular period of free time, and Oliver points out that the playwright describes *The Lover's Melancholy* as the "account of some leisurable hours."[2] Another argument for an early date depends upon the play's versification: several Ford scholars have demonstrated statistically that both *'Tis Pity She's a Whore* and *Love's Sacrifice* have appreciably fewer lines with feminine endings and many more rhyming couplets than the other plays.[3] To determine order of composition by means of stylistic evidence is precarious, however; many factors besides chronology affect style. An objection often raised against the priority of *'Tis Pity* is the relatively early date (1628) for the licensing of *The Lover's Melancholy*. This fact is not, of course, incontrovertible proof of an earlier composition date for the last-mentioned play; but, in view of the paucity of information about the chronology of Ford's works, it can hardly be ignored.

No source is known for the plot of *'Tis Pity She's a Whore*.

Scholars have cited previous stories about incest between brother and sister, but these contain no pronounced similarities to the play and must be regarded as no more than analogues.[4] Of all preceding works, Shakespeare's *Romeo and Juliet* seems most influential, thought not, of course, because of incest; Ford's characterizations of Friar Bonaventura and Putana seem patterned after those of Friar Lawrence and the nurse.[5] Ford in some of his other plays shows an interest in brother-sister relationships, and in *The Broken Heart* Bassanes wrongly accuses Ithocles and Penthea of incest. If Ford wrote *The Broken Heart* before *'Tis Pity*, then the former drama no doubt influenced the latter one.

In *'Tis Pity She's a Whore,* Giovanni confides to Friar Bonaventura that he loves his sister, Annabella. The friar, who warns the youth that only tragedy will result from incest and that "death waits on thy lust," advises him to renounce such sin. But Giovanni, despite prayers and "daily fasts," cannot stifle his passion. He voices it to his sister, offers her his dagger, and says that either she must love him or he must die. Annabella confesses that she reciprocates his passion, and the two become secret lovers. When Soranzo and Bergetto, two young men of Parma, seek to marry Annabella, she, of course, does not encourage their advances. Soranzo, a nobleman, is further occupied in trying to placate his former mistress, Hippolita, who is furiously jealous and accuses him of having ruined her marriage and then abandoning her. As for Bergetto, this goodhearted simpleton soon loses interest in Annabella when he falls in love with Philotis, the niece of Annabella's physician, Richardetto; Richardetto also turns out to be none other than the disguised and vengeful husband of the seduced Hippolita. Annabella's aloofness toward suitors has to end, however, when she becomes pregnant; and, when she repents to the friar of her incest, she accepts his advice to marry Soranzo. Meanwhile, two plots to murder Soranzo fail disastrously: poor Bergetto, mistaken for Soranzo in the darkness by Grimaldi, an assassin hired by Richardetto, is fatally stabbed; the jilted Hippolita, planning to murder Soranzo at his wedding feast, is tricked by his servant Vasques into drinking her own poison and dies in agony while cursing the marriage of Soranzo and Annabella.

brother sister (relationship)

Hippolita's curse is soon realized, for Soranzo learns of his wife's pregnancy and, dragging Annabella by the hair, threatens to kill her if she will not name her lover. When she adamantly and scornfully refuses, Soranzo's crafty servant Vasques persuades him to control his wrath and then elicits from Putana, Annabella's maid, the information that her secret lover is Giovanni. Soranzo, to obtain vengeance, invites Giovanni to a banquet where hired *banditti* are to slay him after he has visited his sister in her chamber. Despite a warning from Annabella written in her own blood, Soranzo's invitation is defiantly accepted by Giovanni, who, unlike his penitent sister, has refused to admit to Friar Bonaventura that incest has been sinful. Going to Annabella's chamber, Giovanni finds her lying on a bed in her bridal robes. Still the lover, he suspects her of "night-games" with Soranzo; but she soon convinces him not only of her love but of their imminent death. Asking Annabella to kiss him and extolling her "most lovely beauty," Giovanni stabs her to death. Then, her heart upon his dagger, he enters the banquet room, informs the astonished guests of what he has done, kills Soranzo, and is slain by Soranzo's henchmen.

As we might expect, the play's topic of incest has occasioned varied responses and interpretations. Some commentators have felt that Ford portrays incest too sympathetically by making Giovanni and Annabella attractive; some even see the playwright as flaunting the conventions of society and as being decadent. Others, however, view Ford as essentially conservative, for Giovanni and Annabella do pay for their love with their lives. But surely, as N. W. Bawcutt contends,[6] the play falls between these two extremes. On the one hand, Giovanni has great dramatic appeal, some of the friar's arguments and actions seem ineffectual, the nurse's coarseness makes Annabella's incest seem almost virtuous, and Soranzo—because of his previous adultery with Hippolita—arouses little compassion in us as the wronged husband of Annabella. On the other hand, Giovanni is not to be taken as Ford's spokesman, his arguments (to the friar) for incest are patently specious, his love becomes tainted with jealousy, and eventually he is guilty of atheism and of murder. Annabella is more sensitive and less selfish than her brother, but her penitence is vitiated both by her insolence toward her husband and by her continued acceptance of her brother as her lover. In other words, Ford portrays the incestuous lovers with understanding, but he does not condone their actions.

II   *Decadence?*

Decadence in *'Tis Pity She's a Whore* depends largely upon the attitude of the reader. If he finds any portrayal of incest offensive, no excellence of the drama will redeem it in his eyes. But many have admired the play for its daring and its directness; the work may be sensational, but it is honest. Before the first act is over, Ford has committed himself to tragedy; and most of the play presents the disastrous consequences of the incest. A comparison with *A King and No King,* an earlier drama by Beaumont and Fletcher, shows Ford's work to be much less prurient. A tragicomedy, *A King and No King* has for its central story the love between King Arbaces of Iberia and his supposed sister, Panthea. Not until the last scene do the lovers (and the audience) learn that they are not related and hence not guilty of incestuous passion. The suspense of the play consists entirely of this concern, which is expertly sustained by the authors.

King Arbaces, who has not seen his sister for several years, intends to marry her to King Tigranes of Armenia, whom he has captured in battle. Before brother and sister meet, Panthea shows excessive interest in her brother's well-being (II.i). When Arbaces meets her (III.i), he is for a long time strangely speechless; then he arbitrarily and vehemently denies that she is his sister. Unable to master his hidden passion for Panthea, Arbaces summons, first, the loyal captain Mardonius and, next, the servile courtier Bessus and asks each to be his pander (III.iii); Mardonius indignantly refuses, but Bessus accepts with such relish that Arbaces is disgusted and dismisses him. When brother and sister again meet (IV.iv), Arbaces tells Panthea that he desires her; she expresses shock, though eventually telling him that, if she were not his sister, she would gladly marry him, and adding "I feel a sin growing upon my blood,/ Worse than all these, hotter, I fear, than yours"; the two decide to separate before they succumb to their passion. Finally (V.iv), Arbaces learns that Panthea is not his sister, and all ends well.

Although Ford probably knew the earlier play and could have
been influenced by it, the purpose of the above summary is
simply to show a significant difference in the aims of the two
dramas, a significance not at all unflattering to Ford. Beaumont
and Fletcher toy with the notion of incest and encourage the
same attitude in their audience; yet, because of the discovery
of Panthea's true parentage in the final scene, they never have
to come to grips with their topic. Such titillation characterizes
much Fletcherian tragicomedy, for the suspense is often a prolonged but unfulfilled anticipation of seduction or revenge. In
this sense, Ford in *'Tis Pity* is, at least to me, less meretricious
and less decadent. When, in the opening line of Act II, Giovanni
says, "Come, Annabella: no more sister now," there can be no
doubt that incestuous love has been consummated. Ford in his
first act encompasses what Beaumont and Fletcher expand to
five acts.

An audience familiar with *A King and No King* must have
found Ford's second scene breathtaking. Already Giovanni has
defended incest to the friar (I.i); and Annabella, seeing her
brother from the window, has asked Putana, "What blessed
shape/ Of some celestial creature now appears?" (I.ii) when
Giovanni dismisses the nurse and begins one of the most suspenseful dialogues in English drama:

>   GIO. Come, sister, lend your hand, let's walk together.
>   I hope you need not blush to walk with me;
>   Here's none but you and I.
>   ANNA. How's this?
>   GIO. Faith, I mean no harm.
>   ANNA. Harm?
>   GIO. No, good faith; how is't with 'ee?
>   ANNA. [*aside*]. I trust he be not frantic. [*To him.*] I am
>   very well, brother.
>   GIO. Trust me, but I am sick, I fear so sick
>   'Twill cost my life.
>   ANNA. Mercy forbid it! 'Tis not so, I hope.
>   GIO. I think you love me, sister.
>   ANNA. Yes, you know I do.
>   GIO. I know't indeed.—Y'are very fair. (I.ii)

Giovanni's utterance of "fair" breaks his restraint, and for the next twenty lines he sensually extols Annabella's beauty: her forehead is fairer than Juno's; her eyes are stars with Promethean fire; her cheeks recall the lily and the rose; her lips would tempt a saint; her hands would "make an anchorite lascivious." When Annabella fends off this praise with gentle scoffing, Giovanni offers her his dagger, confesses his love, and concludes, "Must I now live, or die?" In *A King and No King* Panthea, being similarly approached by Arbaces (IV.iv), states, in a tone of revulsion and righteousness, her preference for death. But Annabella replies: "Live: thou hast won/ The field, and never fought." Brother and sister kneel to vow their love, then kiss. When Giovanni asks, "What must we do now?" Annabella replies, "What you will"; and he ends the scene, as they leave, saying, "Let's learn to court in smiles, to kiss, and sleep."

The play's forcefulness is not confined to its first act. Incest remains a burning issue, and Giovanni continues to be a compelling protagonist whose attitudes and actions are central. In these respects, *'Tis Pity She's a Whore* probably is Ford's greatest drama; for both *The Broken Heart* and *Perkin Warbeck*, its only serious rivals, do not have such intensity. The characterization of Warbeck ultimately lacks completeness because his own view of his imposture is never clarified. Ford's ambiguity doubtless is wise, for to depict Perkin either as a mental case or as a calculating liar would destroy his admirable qualities. But despite the playwright's adroit emphasis and timing, and despite his double image of the titular character as noble Stoic and incompetent statesman, for many readers the unanswered question of Warbeck's thoughts about himself is bothersome. In *The Broken Heart* Ithocles, like Warbeck and Giovanni, is an attractive and presumptuous young man whose aspirations result in tragedy. The causal relationship between Ithocles's character and his death, however, is less immediate than with Giovanni. Ithocles dies because of his arrogant treatment of his sister Penthea, but this misdeed—breaking her betrothal to Orgilus and marrying her to Bassanes—has occurred before the play begins. The Ithocles whom we hear and see addresses his sister with contrition; any brashness he displays concerns his love for

Princess Calantha, which has no logical connection with his earlier selfishness toward Penthea. Thus, for dramatic effectiveness, the role of Ithocles cannot match that of Giovanni.

As a protagonist, Giovanni contributes much to *'Tis Pity She's a Whore,* for by both word and deed he defiantly and amorously perpetuates incest until his death. During his conversations with Friar Bonaventura, they, in their three meetings (I.i, II.v, and V.iii), continue the same debate: the friar asserts that incest is prohibited by Heaven; Giovanni maintains that it is sanctioned by Nature. This argument is never resolved, because Giovanni, unlike Annabella, does not admit to sinfulness or become penitent; hence the play contains a prolonged intellectual, or ethical, tension that many observers or readers probably have found more disconcerting than the physical violence of the several murders.

Giovanni sustains the incest not only by argumentation but by passion, for he is an ardent and a demanding lover—a fact we are not allowed to forget. He is, for example, possessive:

> GIO. But I shall lose you, sweetheart.
> ANNA.   But you shall not.
> GIO. You must be married, mistress.
> ANNA.   Yes? To whom?
> GIO. Someone must have you.
> ANNA.   You must.
> GIO.   Nay, some other.
>   (II.i)

So he asks Annabella to swear she will be his alone, and she complies. Later, when she shows him a jewel that Donado, Bergetto's uncle, has given her (II.vi), he tells her to return it; when she flippantly rejects Soranzo's marriage proposal, he is an interested and reassured eavesdropper (III.ii). At her wedding feast, he cannot bear to "see [his] love/ Clipp'd by another" and refuses to drink a toast to Soranzo and his bride (IV.i).

His passion for Annabella also dominates their final meeting, for, when he enters her chamber and finds her lying on her bed and dressed in her "bridal robes," his initial reaction is one of suspicion and jealousy:

> What, chang'd so soon? Hath your new sprightly lord
> Found out a trick in night-games more than we
> Could know in our simplicity? Ha! Is't so?
> Or does the fit come on you, to prove treacherous
> To your past vows and oaths? (V.v)

When she reprimands him for jesting in the face of calamity, he replies, "What danger's half so great as thy revolt?" Although this remark might at first seem merely a lover's customary hyperbole, its literal truth for Giovanni becomes apparent in their ensuing conversation: to him, their love is everything. Realizing that their deaths are imminent, they discuss the life to come. While Giovanni remains skeptical, Annabella affirms her religious faith; then he voices his deepest concern:

> But d'ee think
> That I shall see you there?—You look on me?
> May we kiss one another, prate or laugh,
> Or do as we do here?

Having decided to kill her, he calls her "fair Annabella," cites her "matchless beauty," asks her to kiss him, then fatally stabs her. As she is dying, he praises her charms: "To dispute/ With thy (even in thy death) most lovely beauty,/ Would make me stagger to perform this act." And, in the next and last scene, Giovanni, mortally wounded by Soranzo's assassins, utters these final words: "Where'er I go, let me enjoy this grace,/ Freely to view my Annabella's face" (V.vi).

III *Vengeance upon Vengeance*

'Tis Pity She's a Whore is a tale of blood as well as of lust; the violent action of this revenge play augments the shock and outrage of its incest. Grimaldi and Vasques duel (I.ii); Bergetto is murdered (III.vii); Hippolita dies of poison (IV.i); Soranzo drags Annabella by the hair (IV.iii); Putana's eyes are put out (IV.iii); and Giovanni kills Annabella (V.v), tears out her heart, kills Soranzo, and is slain (V.vi). Revenge appears in some of Ford's other plays—*The Broken Heart, Love's Sacrifice,* and *The Lady's Trial*—but in none of them is it presented so fully and

so sensationally. And we should note that in the spectacular final scene Ford makes Giovanni his principal character not only as a lover but as an avenger. To have an incestuous adulterer seek vengeance upon the cuckolded husband surely is a remarkable variation on a familiar theme, but the playwright makes it credible; the same impulsiveness, daring, and selfishness that have motivated the lover account for the murderer.

Revenge and its concomitant violence are not limited to this one scene and one character, however. The greater part of the second and third acts deals with two other revenge plots (by Richardetto and by Hippolita), both of them aimed at Soranzo. These secondary stories have several functions: they establish an atmosphere of violence without which the final scene would be too obtrusive, too unexpectedly horrendous for any audience; they alienate us from Soranzo, whom Giovanni is to kill; and they provide Ford with material for the middle of his play—that is, the period between the beginning of incest (II.i) and Soranzo's discovery of his wife's pregnancy (IV.iii).

In one story Richardetto, the disguised husband of Hippolita, plans to kill Soranzo, who has seduced his wife. He persuades the soldier Grimaldi, a rival of Soranzo for the hand of Annabella, to assassinate him, and gives Grimaldi some deadly poison for the point of his rapier. Grimaldi lies in wait, but in the darkness he mistakes the innocent Bergetto for Soranzo and kills him. Bergetto vividly describes his sensations: "O help, help! Here's a stitch fallen in my guts, O for a flesh-tailor quickly! . . . I am sure I cannot piss forward and backward, and yet I am wet before and behind. . . . O my belly seethes like a porridge-pot, some cold water, I shall boil over else; my whole body is in a sweat, that you may wring my shirt; feel here. . . . Is all this mine own blood? Nay, then, good night with me" (III.vii). When the slain Bergetto's uncle, Donado, seeks justice from the cardinal, to whom Grimaldi has gone for protection, the cardinal arrogantly dismisses him (III.ix). As Florio (the father of Giovanni and Annabella) disgustedly concludes, "Justice is fled to Heaven and comes no nearer."

In the other secondary story, Hippolita, a jilted mistress since Soranzo has been courting Annabella, berates him for seduction and desertion, then endeavors to induce his servant, Vasques,

to join her against him (II.ii). At the subsequent wedding banquet of Soranzo and Annabella (IV.i), Hippolita drinks a cup
of wine to their happiness; but, when Soranzo asks for another
cup to return the pledge, Vasques stops him, explaining that
Hippolita has just taken the poison she had intended for the
bridegroom. Dying in agony, Hippolita changes her marriage
blessing to a curse:

> I feel my minute coming. Had that slave
> Kept promise (O, my torment!), thou this hour
> Hadst died, Soranzo—heat above hell fire!—
> Yet ere I pass away—cruel, cruel flames!—
> Take here my curse amongst you; may thy bed
> Of marriage be a rack unto thy heart,
> Burn blood and boil in vengeance—O my heart,
> My flame's intolerable!—Mayst thou live
> To father bastards, may her womb bring forth
> Monsters, and die together in your sins,
> Hated, scorn'd, and unpitied!—O!—O!— (IV.i)

The stunned observers agree with Vasques that he has "fitted
her a just payment in her own coin." All exclaim, "Wonderful
justice!" and Richardetto adds, "Heaven, thou art righteous."
In Bergetto's death justice has been violated, but in Hippolita's
it has been fulfilled. Both instances are relevant to the play's
final scene, as we shall see.

By the third scene of Act IV, Soranzo has discovered that
Annabella is pregnant; consequently, Ford now shifts to his
main story for additional revenge and violence. The enraged
husband enters, dragging Annabella by the hair. Vowing to kill
her if she does not name her lover, he calls her "harlot, rare,
notable harlot," "whore of whores," "excellent quean," "damnable
monster." Because earlier (III.vi) Annabella has penitently confessed her sins to Friar Bonaventura and, upon his advice, agreed
to marry Soranzo, we might expect her to display some contrition toward her husband. She does just the opposite, taunting
him, praising her secret lover, and daring Soranzo to kill her.
In view of Annabella's previous and later (V.i) penitence to
the friar, as well as her sober attitude toward Giovanni in the
last act (V.v), some commentators have felt that Ford has sacri-

ficed consistency of characterization for good theater; indeed, in
Love's Sacrifice Bianca addresses her threatening husband in the
same sensational manner (V.i). In this connection, we should
also note that *'Tis Pity*, like *Romeo and Juliet*, takes place in
Italy, where, according to popular opinion in Elizabethan and
Stuart England, the most terrible and spectacular deeds occurred. More than once Ford reminds us of the setting: Annabella sings Italian lyrics as Soranzo physically attacks her
(III.vi), and Vasques pays Soranzo the highest compliment as a
bloodthirsty avenger when he says, "Now you begin to turn
Italian" (V.iv).

As Act IV draws to a close, Vasques becomes a major figure
in the revenge story; and he remains one for the rest of the
play. Cunning, ruthless, and, in his own sinister style, zestful,
he seeks, and almost obtains, full vengeance for Soranzo. First,
he coaxes Putana into identifying Annabella's lover. No sooner
has the nurse named Giovanni than Vasques summons his
banditti: "Come, sirs, take me this old damnable hag, gag her
instantly, and put out her eyes. . . . Let me come to her; I'll
help your old gums, you toad-bellied bitch. Sirs, carry her
closely into the coalhouse, and put out her eyes instantly; if
she roars, slit her nose: d'ee hear, be speedy and sure. Why,
this is excellent and above expectation" (IV.iii).

Imparting his information to Soranzo, Vasques also goads his
master to frenzy: "A cuckold is a goodly tame beast, my lord"
and "Think upon incest and cuckoldry" (V.ii). Although Soranzo
conceives of having Annabella "deck herself in all her bridal
robes," of inviting Giovanni to a birthday feast, and of readying
the *banditti* in ambush (V.ii), it is Vasques who originates the
devilish scheme of murdering Giovanni in the act of incest and
hence damning his soul: "—when my young incest-monger comes,
he will be sharp set on his old bit: give him time enough, let
him have your chamber and bed at liberty; let my hot hare
have law ere he be hunted to his death, that if it be possible,
he may post to hell in the very act of his damnation" (V.iv).
The trap, then, has been set. Giovanni is to be apprehended
(the watchword for the *banditti* is "Vengeance!") and slain in
his sister's bed; and the banquet guests, including the cardinal,
are unknowingly to be witnesses of the incest and thereby ex-

onerate Soranzo. But, like Hippolita and Richardetto, Soranzo is destined to lose at the game of revenge.

In the final act of *'Tis Pity She's a Whore,* the principal avenger is not Vasques or Soranzo but Giovanni. Ford has prepared us for this tour de force: we feel no sympathy for Soranzo as a wronged husband, for he has ruined the marriage of Richardetto and Hippolita, mistreated his own wife, and helped plan the murder of Giovanni; Soranzo is also degraded by his association with the brutal, heartless Vasques. Furthermore, we must find Giovanni hardly culpable as an avenger because he has been forced into his desperate role: immediately after the friar has brought him a letter from Annabella, written in her blood and telling him they are discovered, Vasques enters with an invitation to Soranzo's banquet; the murderous intent is manifest. Our protagonist accepts the challenge:

> GIO. Yes, tell him I dare come.
> VASQUES. "Dare come"?
> GIO. So I said; and tell him more, I will come.
> VASQUES. These words are strange to me.
> GIO. Say I will come.
> VASQUES. You will not miss?
> GIO. Yet more? I'll come! Sir, are you answered?
> VASQUES. So I'll say.—My service to you. (V.iii)

Vasques having departed, the friar implores Giovanni not to go, warning him that his life will be in danger. But Giovanni has taken up the gauntlet of revenge: "Not go? Yes, and re-solve/ To strike as deep in slaughter as they all./ For I will go." Although the friar leaves in despair, we react with awe rather than revulsion at such an impetuous and death-defying commitment. And as Giovanni leaves for the banquet, his last words indicate that he will be no passive victim: "If I must totter like a well-grown oak,/ Some under-shrubs shall in my weighty fall/ Be crush'd to splits: with me thy all shall perish" (V.iii).

Giovanni and Annabella see each other for the last time (V.v) in a meeting as long and as sensational as their first one (I.ii); then Giovanni initiated their incest, but now he terminates it. In brilliant fashion, the playwright fuses his two themes of lust and revenge into an unforgettable love-death that is emblematized by Annabella's heart. Giovanni visits his sister, who tells him they are to be murdered; he praises their love and Annabella's beauty, then says that he is going to kill her. Three times he asks for a kiss; during their third embrace, he stabs her "To save thy fame, and kill thee in a kiss./ Thus die, and die by me, and by my hand!/ Revenge is mine; honor doth love command." Thus Annabella dies, slain not by a murderous husband but by a lover who, even as she dies, amorously extols her "most lovely beauty." Already the ingenious scheme of Soranzo and Vasques has failed, but Giovanni the avenger has much more to do.

In the banquet chamber (V.vi), Soranzo, though hospitable to his guests, is about to spring his trap on the lovers. But he never does; Giovanni enters, with a heart on his dagger, and, in the stunned silence, describes himself as "proud in the spoil/ Of love and vengeance" and alludes to "the rape of life and beauty" that he has just enacted. On his dagger, he explains, is Annabella's heart. He then states that for nine months he has been his sister's lover and is the father of her unborn child. The cardinal is shocked, and Giovanni's father, Florio, is incredulous; Soranzo is enraged: "I shall burst with fury;/ Bring the strumpet forth." Vasques goes to the chamber and returns to verify Giovanni's story; Florio drops dead from shock. But Giovanni is not deterred; turning upon Soranzo, he fatally stabs him: "Soranzo, see this heart, which was thy wife's;/ Thus I exchange it royally for thine, [*Stabs him.*]/ And thus and thus! Now brave revenge is mine."

Vasques comes to his master's aid and also calls the *banditti*, who rush in to overpower Giovanni. But Sorenzo, though glad to see his "wrongs reveng'd on that black devil," dies first. The cardinal instructs the mortally wounded Giovanni to "call for mercy" and "cry to Heaven"; the latter scorns him: "Mercy? Why, I have found it in this justice." So does Giovanni triumph in death. And we recall how Ford's denouement was foreshadowed by the two earlier revenge episodes. Soranzo, like Hippolita, deserves to be slain because he has plotted murder. Giovanni, unlike Bergetto's uncle, Donado, seeks justice not from the cardinal but by his own avenging dagger.

Something more should be said about the structure of *'Tis*

Pity She's a Whore. Although the subplots establish an atmosphere of revenge, divorce our sympathies from Soranzo, and present a double view of justice, they have little direct connection with the main story. Of the four plays already discussed, *'Tis Pity,* in my opinion, has the loosest construction. In *The Lover's Melancholy,* the two principal stories are joined by the device of disguise (Eroclea as Parthenophil), while the main plot, centered on Palador and Meleander, is presented in a series of six alternating scenes; in *The Broken Heart,* the two tragedies of Orgilus and Penthea and of Ithocles and Calantha are closely linked by plot, song, and spectacle, and there is no subplot; in *Perkin Warbeck,* the first half of the play consists of nine scenes alternating between Henry in England and Warbeck and James in Scotland, the second half depicts a politically defeated but personally courageous protagonist, and again there is no subplot.

In contrast is *'Tis Pity.* For example, we have Ford's handling of Bergetto: although this character's death contributes vividness and sensationalism to the play, most of the time his role is ineffectual. In the first three acts, Bergetto appears in no less than six scenes and is prominent in each of them; but only in the last one (in which he dies) is he memorable. In the others, whether talking to his uncle, his servant, Annabella, Florio, Philotis, or Richardetto, he seems intended as a comical booby who is more interested in seeing a mill operated by sandbags or a horse with its head just behind its tail (I.iii) than in courting Annabella; he proves more tiresome than funny and does not serve as an effective parallel or foil to either Giovanni or Soranzo. Nor is the Hippolita story assimilated into the play any more thoroughly; the masque whereby she introduces herself at the wedding feast seems superfluous.

Muriel Bradbrook, who finds no connection between the play's comic and serious characters, compares it unfavorably with Middleton's *Women, Beware Women.*[7] Madeleine Doran states, "The essentially episodic character of the plotting is concealed by a specious appearance of complication; specious because the chain of complication involving Richardetto-Hippolita-Grimaldi-Soranzo-Bergetto has nothing really to do with the main issue, the love of Annabella and her brother."[8]

CHAPTER 8

Lust and No Lust: Love's Sacrifice

I *The Story and Its Sources*

A DRAMA in many ways similar to *'Tis Pity* and, like it, published in 1633 and performed by the Queen's company is *Love's Sacrifice.*[1] Both in style and in content the two works seem quite close; therefore, whichever was earlier must have had considerable influence on the other. Lust and revenge are prominent in both, and the two heroines—Annabella and Bianca—are noticeably similar when confronting their enraged husbands. For the main story of *Love's Sacrifice* no source is known; Sargeaunt has noted a parallel between the Ferentes subplot and Sidney's *Arcadia,*[2] and Davril finds an analogue in Heywood's *A Woman Killed with Kindness,* in which another husband returns home to find his wife in the arms of his best friend.[3] The play also reminds us of *Othello*, especially when the Iago-like D'Avolos is persuading the Duke of Pavia that his wife is an adulteress. Though not the equal of *'Tis Pity, The Broken Heart,* or *Perkin Warbeck, Love's Sacrifice* is a tragedy of merit; we suspect that, like the tragicomedy *The Lover's Melancholy,* it deserves a better reputation.

In the play, Philippo Caraffa, Duke of Pavia and husband of the beautiful Bianca, is visited by Fernando, his closest friend. The duke's sister, Fiormonda, conceives a violent passion for Fernando, but her advances (made by her confidant D'Avolos) are rejected by him. Fernando's coolness is explained by his having fallen in love with the duchess; when he tells her, Bianca rebukes him and threatens to inform her husband. Also at the court is Ferentes, a "wanton courtier" who has seduced three women: Julia, Colona, and Morona. Each has been given his promise of marriage, and each is with child. Learning of his promiscuity, they gain vengeance by murdering Ferentes during a masque.

As for Fernando, his secret passion for Bianca is detected by D'Avolos, who notes his enraptured comments on a portrait of the duchess. D'Avolos's suspicions, which he reports to Fiormonda, are confirmed when he witnesses Fernando kneeling before Bianca and holding her hand. But D'Avolos has not heard their conversation in which Bianca has once more chastised Fernando and in which the latter has pledged never to woo her again. That night Bianca unexpectedly visits Fernando in his bedchamber; and, to his joy, she offers herself to him. There is, however, one proviso: if he gratifies his desire, she will kill herself. Fernando renounces his "wanton appetite," and the two exchange chaste kisses; they will be lovers, but with no physical consummation.

Meanwhile, D'Avolos and Fiormonda, convinced of Bianca's adultery, rouse the duke to jealous fury. The latter informs his wife that he is going to Lucca; but, remaining in Pavia, he breaks into Bianca's chamber to find her kissing Fernando. Believing his suspicions confirmed, he has guards take away Fernando, then accuses his wife of adultery. When she refuses to exonerate herself, he stabs her to death. Only later, when Fernando refuses to fight and insists that he and Bianca have committed no "actual folly," does the duke realize that Bianca is not an adulteress. Grief-stricken, he buries her; as he is taking a "last farewell," the tomb opens, and Fernando emerges in a winding sheet. He reiterates his love for Bianca and proclaims their innocence, drinks a vial of poison, and dies. The duke, lamenting the loss of his friend as well as his wife, fatally stabs himself.

The key word in *Love's Sacrifice* is *lust;* other frequently used ones are *adultery* and *cuckold.* All three signify illicit sexual intercourse, which is the unforgivable sin in Ford's Pavia, one which merits bloody retribution. Any extramarital indiscretion other than lust ("actual folly") may be dismissed as "trivial wantonness." The amorous words and the kisses of Bianca and

Fernando (V.i) should be so judged, because the two are adhering to their secret vow of continence; but the duke, already convinced of adultery, mistakenly regards their actions as evidence of "lust" and kills his wife. Herein lies the tragedy, as well as the dominant point of view, of the play.

Some Ford scholars have criticized the story as implausible; and others, who have offered a different interpretation, regard Bianca as a vow-breaker responsible for the tragedy.[4] Still others have charged that the work is imitative of earlier dramas, or that Ford is guilty of cutting corners and of sacrificing too much for a spectacular ending. *Love's Sacrifice,* however, reveals a purposive rather than a drifting playwright. Possibly his goal is ill-chosen or is too difficult to achieve, but it is carefully stated; Ford's presentation of his thesis is worth examining.

II   *Two Pointers: Ferentes and D'Avolos*

A helpful guide is Ferentes, whose amorous exploits exemplify the play's concept of *lust* and whose death informs us that lust deserves murder. This code is the one by which we and the duke are to judge Bianca and Fernando. In the first scene, Ferentes is described as one "whose pride takes pride/ In nothing more than to delight his lust." In the second scene, he arranges assignations, first with Colona, "In the grove; good sweet, remember; in any case alone,—d'ye mark, love?—not as much as your duchess' little dog," and next with Julia, "I'll meet thee soon in thy lady's back-lobby, I will, wench; look for me." After each woman has left, he comments cynically of chastity: "He that is not a cuckold or a bastard is a strangely happy man; for a chaste wife, or a mother that never stepped awry, are wonders, wonders in Italy" and "Chastity! . . . I never found it in a woman thoroughly tempted yet."

The function of Ferentes becomes even clearer in his two appearances in Act III. In the first of these (III.i), which immediately follows the bedchamber scene in which Bianca and Fernando vow continence, Ferentes is preceded on the stage by Colona and Julia, both of whom confess to their fathers, Nibrassa and Petruchio, respectively, that they are pregnant by Ferentes. Nibrassa calls Colona "whore," "strumpet," and "leprosy of my blood" and refers to Ferentes as a "lecher" and "smooth devil"; in Act V, the duke also uses such terms in describing Bianca and Fernando. The two fathers and daughters draw aside as Ferentes enters with a third victim, Morona. She calls him "unconscionable villain" and a "perjured, damnable, ungracious defiler of women"; he responds with "tough carrion hen" and "jennet." When Julia and Colona come forward to join Morona in upbraiding their seducer, he calls them "three Flanders mares" and departs.

Ferentes's crimes are punished in the final scene of Act III. In a masque given for the visiting Abbot of Monaco, the three women surround Ferentes, then stab him. They re-enter, unmasked, each with a child in her arms; these infants are, as Julia explains, "pledges of this false man's lust"; here, in contrast to the Bianca murder scene (V.i), the evidence of sexual intercourse is incontrovertible. The dying Ferentes exclaims: "Pox upon all cod–piece extravagancy! . . . My forfeit was in my blood; and my life hath answered it." The abbot ends the scene by sanctioning the punishment: "Here's fatal sad presages: but 'tis just/ He dies by murder that hath liv'd in lust." We are to regard, therefore, the slaying of Ferentes as justifiable homicide. By the same token, we must agree that if, later in the play, Bianca is really an adulteress, the duke has the right to murder her. But she is innocent; and therefore the duke, because of his own flaw, jealousy, commits a terrible wrong.

Ford indicates in additional ways the purpose and pattern of his drama. One useful device is D'Avolos, who repeatedly reminds the duke of his cuckoldry. For example, D'Avolos claims that Bianca "doth so palpably, so apparently make her adulteries a trophy, whiles the poting-stick to her unsatiate and more than goatish abomination jeers at and flouts your sleepish . . . security" (IV.i) and that Fernando "holds it religion to make your own trust a key to open the passage to your own wife's womb, to be drunk in the privacies of your bed!" (IV.i). The induced vision of adultery so preoccupies the duke that, when he discovers Bianca and Fernando embracing (V.i), he at once thinks them guilty.

As we have observed earlier, the goading D'Avolos has often been likened to Iago. There are obvious similarities, but one important difference has been ignored: Iago is completely and knowingly responsible for the lie concerning Desdemona, but D'Avolos is largely a victim of misleading circumstances. Early in the play (II.ii), he observes Fernando "striking his breast" and "tearing his hair," manifest symptoms of "plain passion"; when he shows Fernando a life-like portrait of Bianca, the latter exclaims distractedly "A hair! . . . Lip! . . . Love! Heart!" Describing to Fiormonda this behavior of Fernando, D'Avolos cites "the infinite appetite of lust in the piercing adultery of his eye" (II.ii). D'Avolos is perhaps telling the truth, for these incidents occur before Bianca and Fernando vow continence (II.iv). D'Avolos may also be excused somewhat for misconstruing what he witnesses but does not overhear (III.iii). From behind a curtain, he sees Fernando kneel before Bianca, rise, and kiss her hand; but he does not hear their conversation, in which Fernando claims that his love is chaste, in which Bianca then berates him for "the baseness of [his] lust," and in which Fernando in turn promises never again to declare his love.

Yet, while D'Avolos is much less the liar than Iago, Ford manages to make him seem just as villainous; he produces this effect in various ways. For instance, in the first act we find D'Avolos a schemer in his handling of Roseilli's banishment. Later (IV.ii) we see him as a hypocrite: though condemning lust to the duke, he encourages it in Julia when, wooing her, he minimizes her previous affair with Ferentes: "What though thou have a child,— or perhaps two?" But Ford's chief method of demeaning D'Avolos is to depict him as a cunning manipulator of the duke. Instead of reporting in a forthright manner Bianca's seeming adultery, D'Avolos resorts to innuendo and subsequent grossly sensual imagery. And, by the time the duke has been worked up to murderous frenzy, we have seen so much of his Iago-like confidant that we forget that D'Avolos's reason for his interpretation of the Bianca-Fernando affair was much more excusable than the motives of his Shakespearean counterpart. More significantly, our dislike of D'Avolos late in the play encourages us to side with Bianca and Fernando. We know (after III.iv) that they are not guilty of lust; D'Avolos, by insisting vehemently and vividly that they are, makes us sympathetic toward lovers who only kiss.

Ford prepares for his final act in still another manner. In the

makes it quite clear that the one crucial requisite is avoidance
of sexual intercourse. And we should note in the above passage
Bianca's reference to her conscience; for her remarks about sleeping with Fernando reveal her as technically chaste because her
conscience precludes her fulfilling her desire. Similarly chaste
are the kisses exchanged by the lovers. This restraint, inciden-
tally, distinguishes Bianca's attitude from the passion of Fiormonda, the duke's sister, who has unreservedly sought Fernando's physical love. Both Fernando (IV.ii) and, eventually,
Fiormonda herself (V.iii) describe her attitude as "lust";
Roseilli, even more explicit, warns his friend Fernando:

> Know then, sir, her proud heart
> Is only fix'd on you, in such extremes
> Of violence and passion, that I fear,
> Or she'll enjoy you, or she'll ruin you. (III.ii)

Our recognition of Bianca's innocence is necessary if we are to
perceive the pattern of tragedy envisioned by Ford. If we see
her as guilty, as having somehow broken her pledge of continence, her death no longer is pitiful, and her husband's repentance seems uncalled for. At least one commentator has
pointed an accusing finger at her: she has tried to break the vow;
and this weakness accounts for the ensuing tragedy.[5] Ford, however, does not expect us to judge the embracing Bianca and
Fernando as does the duke, whose view has been distorted by
D'Avolos. But still bothersome is the demand that we condone
amorous words and kisses. Logically, we may admit that these do
not constitute adultery; psychologically, we tend to lessen our
sympathy and to verge toward the duke's feeling of outrage, for
we find the behavior of the lovers difficult to tolerate.

III *D'Avenant's* The Platonic Lovers

The relationship between Bianca and Fernando would not
have so puzzled Ford's audience, who must have regarded their
love as Platonic. Such a conclusion is supported, for example,
by William D'Avenant's *The Platonic Lovers*,[6] a play first printed
in 1636, which, besides reflecting the Neoplatonism flourishing
under Queen Henrietta Maria of England, bears some interest-

ing similarities to *Love's Sacrifice*. My purpose is not to contend
that one play directly influenced the other, or even that Ford
was appreciably affected by the Platonic coterie at the English
court (the latter point has been discussed and debated at length
by others);[7] but what can be asserted is that the code of conduct
in *Love's Sacrifice* was not unique to Ford's contemporaries.

For example, in D'Avenant's play, Theander and Eurithea are
Platonic lovers; another couple, Phylomont (Eurithea's brother)
and Ariola (Theander's sister), are not. Fredeline, a minor character, distinguishes between the two relationships:

> The first are lovers of a pure
> Coelestial kind, such as some style Platonical;
> A new court epithet scarce understood;
> But all they woo, sir, is the spirit, face,
> And heart: therefore their conversation is
> More safe to fame. The other still affect
> For natural ends
> . . . .
> [By] such a way as libertines call lust,
> But peaceful politicks and cold divines
> Name matrimony, Sir; therefore although
> Their wise intent be good and lawful, yet
> Since it infers much game and pleasure i'th' event,
> In subtle bashfulness she would not seem
> To entertain with too much forwardness,
> What she perhaps doth willingly expect. (I.i)

Theander and Eurithea, because they do not seek physical consummation ("lust"), converse more freely and less awkwardly.
Phylomont, being rejected by Ariola when he offers to hold her
hand, complains: "Theander may embrace my sister's hand,/
Until with warmth he melt it from the wrist:/ Why should I
have less am'rous privilege?" Ariola explains: "The meaning of/
Their love is only mutual wonder and applause,/ And so pro-
claim'd; therefore can stir no jealousy/ In the severest thought"
(II.i).

Privileges later taken by the two Platonics are striking: when
Theander unabashedly visits Eurithea at night in her bedchamber and bids her servant Amadine leave, Amadine remarks: "This

is an odd kind of lover. He comes/ Into my lady's chamber at all hours"; later, when Theander is to visit Eurithea, Amadine remarks, "He . . . meets/ Her straight to whine and kiss. That's all they do" (III.i). In Act IV, Ariola secretly decides to become Platonic; and her altered behavior surprises and pleases Phylomont. When he asks her for an explanation—"Why are thy courtesies/ So great now, and so easily attain'd,/ Which heretofore thou didst deprive me of/ With frowns, and strict behaviour of thy brow?"—Ariola replies:

> It shall be ever thus. My passion, and
> My thoughts are chang'd; as Eurithea with
> My brother lives, so shall our conversation take
> All liberty, and our salutes be far
> More amorous and bold, though virtuous still. (IV.i)

An opposite change has occurred in the other love affair. Theander, having unknowingly taken a love philter, marries Eurithea with consummation in mind. When she learns of his purpose she is stunned; conscience-stricken, Theander confesses his error: "Know all/ Our married vows . . . I merely took,/ As formal helps to my pernicious lust" (IV.i).

In *Love's Sacrifice,* the relationship between Bianca and Fernando is handled somewhat differently by Ford since their vow of continence is secret. Theander can, without suspicion, embrace Eurithea and visit her in her bedchamber because they are known to be Platonic lovers; when Fernando is discovered in a similar situation with Bianca, the result is tragedy. Nevertheless, a similar viewpoint obtains in both plays: if two lovers renounce coition, they may indulge in "lesser" pleasures. Therefore Bianca and Fernando are to consider themselves innocent; and a seventeenth-century audience, more familiar with Platonic and pseudo-Platonic stances than we, would have readily discerned Ford's intention.

Also puzzling to some readers is Bianca's unrepentant, almost flaunting response to her husband's accusations of adultery (V.i). Since the duke indicates that lust is what damns her in his eyes —he calls her "wretched whore," "strumpet," and "shameless harlot" and refers to her "cursèd womb,/ In which the mixture of that traitor's lust/ Impostumes for a birth of bastardy"—why does she not directly deny his charges? Instead, she extols at length Fernando's handsomeness. We could argue that Bianca's reaction is implausible and that Ford, desiring a spectacular, violent finale of murder and suicide, sacrifices consistency of characterization for good theater. He seems trapped by his plot: Bianca must simultaneously keep her husband angry enough to kill her yet retain her innocence.

On the other hand, the playwright must be given credit for having foreseen this dilemma and prepared his audience for Bianca's harsh reply; and he has done so principally in two ways. In the preceding act (IV.ii), the duke informs Bianca of his suspicion by relating a dream to her (Fernando has clapped the cuckold's horns on the duke's head), and he threatens murder. Bianca briefly asserts but does not argue her innocence: "Did such a guilt/ Hang on mine honour, 'twere no blame in you,/ If you did stab me to the heart." Because in this incident Bianca not only becomes aware of her husband's jealousy but realizes the futility of trying to reason with him, her response in the next act is more understandable. Also, Bianca is a woman of pride as well as integrity; she has done nothing to be ashamed of, and the duke's accusations are insulting. Ford's other device appeals more to our reason than to our emotions: Bianca, in praising Fernando to her husband, reminds him that if she has been influenced by natural attraction she is no guiltier than he: "The self-same appetite which led you on/ To marry me led me to love your friend" (V.i). That the duke has chosen Bianca for her great beauty is stated explicitly in Act I by both Petruchio and the duke himself.

During this final conversation between husband and wife (V.i), we are reminded more than once that only adultery requires vengeance. The duke says to Bianca: "Can you imagine you have so much art/ Which may persuade me you and your close marksman/ Did not a little traffic in my right?" Any lesser indiscretion he will forgive: "'Tis not the tide/ Of trivial wantonness from youth to youth,/ But thy abusing of thy lawful bed,/ Thy husband's bed." And, even when Bianca refuses to exonerate herself, he hesitates to kill her, saying "She may live and change." But, pushed by Fiormonda, he asks Bianca for her hand and, as he stabs her, exclaims, "Here's blood for lust."

In the next scene (V.ii), Fernando convinces him of Bianca's innocence. No sooner have the two men met than the duke repeats his accusation: he refers to Fernando's "lust" and, drawing his sword, threatens to "mix your souls together in your deaths,/ As you did both your bodies in her life." Fernando's rebuttal is quick and direct. Dropping his sword, he states, "If the chaste Bianca/ Be murder'd, murder me." This willingness to die, in itself a forceful indication of truthfulness, is followed by a host of attestations to Bianca's virtue: she has been "a wife as free from lust/ As any terms of art can deify"; Fernando never "unshrin'd/ The altar of her purity"; though guilty of "lawless courtship," he is free of "any actual folly"; she has been as chaste "as virtue's self is good." Nibrassa and Petruchio, two respected counselors of state, declare their belief in the statements of Fernando, who in turn swears upon his sword. Confronted with such overwhelming conviction, the duke exclaims "Bianca chaste!" and attempts to kill himself.

A few more comments must be made about the structure of *Love's Sacrifice.* With its two subplots centered on Ferentes and Fiormonda, the play belongs with the more complex, or busier, of Ford's works; it should be grouped with *'Tis Pity She's a Whore* and *The Lover's Melancholy* but not with *The Broken Heart* and *Perkin Warbeck,* which have no secondary stories. The principal similarities between *Love's Sacrifice* and *'Tis Pity* have already been mentioned; those between *Love's Sacrifice* and *The Lover's Melancholy* have not. Easily the most striking is the parallel between the Thamasta and Fiormonda subplots in the two plays. In *The Lover's Melancholy* Thamasta falls violently in love with Parthenophil, has her servant Kala speak to the "youth," then woos him herself, only to be rejected. At the same time, Thamasta scorns the devoted Menaphon but eventually, upon realizing her folly (Parthenophil is Eroclea in disguise), humbly and gladly accepts him; she also receives some attention from the comical courtier Cuculus, who addresses one of his love poems to her. In *Love's Sacrifice* Fiormonda burns with passion for Fernando, has her confidant D'Avolos speak to him, then does so herself; but, like Thamasta, she is rejected. Roseilli is Menaphon's counterpart, for he remains Fiormonda's faithful lover throughout the play and ultimately becomes her husband;

and Mauruccio, with his foolish poems directed at Fiormonda, reminds us of Cuculus.

The likeness between the two plays suggests that one is indebted to the other, but the direction of such influence cannot be ascertained because, as we stated earlier, of the indefinite chronology of Ford's works. In my opinion, the Thamasta story is more effectively assimilated in its drama, chiefly because of the disguise device which unites the curing of Prince Palador and Meleander, the amorous affairs of Thamasta, and even the asinine antics of Cuculus, who believes that his page is a girl. In *Love's Sacrifice*, the Fiormonda subplot seems less firmly linked to the rest of the play. Roseilli's disguise as a fool lacks color and comedy and contributes nothing to the story; and Mauruccio's humor is no more effective, though his poetic conceit of the mirror-heart does prefigure the imagery of Bianca's and Fernando's love vows.

On the other hand, Fiormonda significantly affects the main story. By wooing and being rejected by Fernando early in the play, she makes him seem virtuous to us before we learn of his love for Bianca; Fernando may be fallible (at least until his vow of continence), but he is no rake, and certainly not a Ferentes. Also, Fiormonda in the later scenes adds her strident and jealousy-laden accusations to those of D'Avolos and thereby makes us hostile toward any and all charges—even those uttered by a hapless husband—against Bianca and Fernando.

Although *Love's Sacrifice* does not have the stature of Ford's three other extant tragedies, it should not be underrated—or misinterpreted. This discussion has endeavored to show the author's carefully developed theme based upon *lust*, as well as his assumption in his denouement of some knowledge of Platonic-love conventions. While we must admit that Bianca's physical chastity is less impressive than, let us say, Penthea's spiritual purity in *The Broken Heart*, it seems unfair to regard *Love's Sacrifice* as being excessively imitative or as collapsing after the scene initiating Platonic love (II.iv). And it seems inaccurate to label Bianca a vow-breaker and to hold her responsible for the play's tragedy, or to deny to the work its rather inflexible and awkward moral code simply because it cannot be found in any of Ford's other plays.

CHAPTER 9

The Fancies Chaste and Noble
and The Lady's Trial

O F Ford's seven plays, the two with the slightest reputations are *The Fancies Chaste and Noble* and *The Lady's Trial.*[1] These two tragicomedies—some prefer to view *The Fancies* as a comedy—probably were the last to be written, since both were entered in the Stationers' Register in 1638; but Ewing, seeing ridicule of *The Fancies* in Shirley's *Changes* (licensed in 1631/32), suggests that it may have been written much earlier than is generally thought.[2] In both dramas Ford appears to experiment, to create variations on the revenge theme depicted so directly and sensationally in *'Tis Pity She's a Whore* and in *Love's Sacrifice.* In *The Fancies,* the playwright resorts to Fletcherian dramaturgy to trick the audience with a surprise ending; in *The Lady's Trial,* he again tells a story that seems headed for tragedy only to end happily—but instead of manipulating plot, he focuses upon the thoughts and discussions of personae to write what Oliver has called "an entirely new kind of psychological drama."[3]

I The Fancies Chaste and Noble

In Sienna, the setting for the action of *The Fancies Chaste and Noble,* Troylo-Savelli, nephew of the Marquis Octavio, urges Livio to accept preferment not only for himself but for his sister, Castamela. Livio, who accedes to his friend's offer, tells

119

both Castamela and her suitor, Romanello, that she will have nothing to fear at Octavio's court, for she will be in the company of three young ladies—Clarella, Silvia, and Floria—known as "the Fancies." When Livio later has misgivings about his sister's welfare, Troylo explains that his uncle is impotent; Castamela is similarly reassured by Morosa, a servant of Octavio.

Elsewhere in Sienna lives Flavia, wife of Lord Julio. Although it is rumored that she has deserted her first husband, Fabricio, she is in truth the injured party; Fabricio contritely admits to her his infidelity, but his guilt is not known by her brother, Romanello, nor by her second husband's two attendants, Camillo and Vespucci, all three of whom consider her a loose woman. Still another object of suspicion is Morosa, whose husband, the barber Secco, has been told by the servant and self-styled eunuch Spadone that she is having an adulterous affair with the page Nitido.

Meanwhile, Romanello fears the corruption of Castamela at Octavio's court, so he readily agrees to the suggestion that he visit the palace disguised as a malcontent; his stay there convinces him that Castamela is an inmate of the marquis's seraglio. Castamela later meets Octavio alone and, though still believing him impotent, upbraids him as a selfish sensualist. Soon, however, she appears quite serene; and her apparent lack of concern enrages her brother, Livio, who now thinks her corrupted. Desperate, Livio goes to Romanello and offers Castamela in marriage, but the disenchanted suitor rejects the proposal.

Romanello does have one consolation: he has learned of his sister Flavia's virtue, as have the attendants Camillo and Vespucci, who shamefacedly admit that they have hoped to seduce their master's seemingly wanton wife. Another misconception is shattered when Spadone states that Secco is not a cuckold, that his charge of Morosa's adultery with Nitido has been a lie; later, when Secco threatens to cut his throat in the barber's chair, Spadone also confesses that he is not a eunuch. Still in doubt, however, is the integrity of Castamela and Octavio. Livio, believing himself betrayed, challenges Troylo to a duel, but his wrath vanishes when he learns the truth: the three young "Fancies" are Octavio's nieces, orphans whom he has raised with great care; and Castamela's visit to court has simply been part of Troylo's scheme to win her as his wife and to induce Romanello to renounce her.

The foregoing summary probably has indicated two aspects of *The Fancies Chaste and Noble* that many a reader has found objectionable: its surprise ending and its prurient tone. We feel that Ford has deliberately tricked us by encouraging unchaste thoughts which the fifth act suddenly reveals as erroneous. Moreover, the title refers only secondarily to Octavio's three young ladies; it pertains chiefly to the unchaste fancies not only of most of the personae but of the reader himself, who until the last minute suspects that the Fancies are not virgins and that the allegedly harmless Octavio is really their lustful corrupter. Keeping an audience in ignorance is not Ford's invention, of course. Jonson, for instance, does so in *Epicoene*, where the supposedly "silent woman" is revealed as garrulous in Act III and as a male in Act V; the hermaphroditical denotation of *epicoene* suddenly acquires additional relevance, as does Ford's title. But Jonson's play, though it may leave a bitter taste about the relationship between sexes, does not make the reader feel prurient. More pertinent, in this respect, are some of Fletcher's plays, such as *A King and No King*, which exploits the audience's secret desire, never finally gratified, for the consummation of incestuous love.

To point out that Ford is not the only playwright guilty of such trickery does not, however, excuse him. Most modern readers find *The Fancies* offensive. On the other hand, the manner in which he achieves his questionable goal is dexterous enough to deserve some attention. But, before discussing the story of Castamela and Octavio, we may profitably consider the function of two minor characters: Flavia and Spadone. Flavia has impressed more than one commentator as the most lifelike and appealing persona of the drama. Often cited is her attempt to conceal from her husband Julio a generous compassion for her former husband, the faithless Fabricio:

> Prithee, sweetest
> Hark in your ear,—beshrew't, the brim of your hat

> Struck in mine eye,—[*Aside*] Dissemble, honest tears,
> The griefs my heart does labour in,—[it] smarts
> Unmeasurably. (III.ii)

One reason for Flavia's dramatic effectiveness is that she is, for the most part, not directly involved in Ford's deception of us—and such is the author's intention. Early in the play (II.i) we learn, long before most of the characters do, that the unflattering rumors about Flavia are false; she is not a wanton who has abandoned a poor merchant for a wealthy lord, but a loyal wife whom Fabricio has sought to pander. Not until Act IV do her brother Romanello and her husband's two attendants, Camillo and Vespucci, learn the truth. Before this discovery, their thoughts about her have been most uncharitable, Camillo and Vespucci going so far as to imagine her capable of adultery with them.

In retrospect, we realize that Ford has purposely given us the right viewpoint for the entire play: the three men have made an erroneous and slanderous judgment based upon inadequate circumstantial evidence; their fancies have not been chaste and noble. The clue is offered to us; and, if we fail to apply it elsewhere, we must confess ourselves as fallible as they. One weakness in Ford's depiction of Flavia is, however, her feigned levity when in the company of Camillo and Vespucci. Although she later explains that such behavior served as protection against their dishonorable aspirations, this reason does not make a great deal of sense to the reader, who finds Ford subordinating his otherwise fine characterization of Flavia to the exigencies of an excessively contrived plot.

The Flavia story proves to be the only reliable pointer in *The Fancies*. It is greatly outnumbered by misleading signs, all of which are uncorrected until the last two acts. The role of Spadone illustrates Ford's use of such deception. Spadone tells two lies: that Morosa has been cuckolding her husband Secco with the page Nitido, and that Spadone himself is a eunuch. He admits the first lie, when questioned before others by the jealous Secco (IV.i), and later (V.ii) the second one, when Secco threatens to cut his throat. Yet Spadone's major contribution is to the main plot, particularly his effect upon our appraisals of the three

Fancies and of their guardian, Octavio. Spadone is foul minded and foulmouthed, whether he is describing his own alleged disability, the marriage of Secco and Morosa, or the young ladies; and, since he speaks early in the play, he gives us initial impressions. Of the Fancies he says: "[They] fumble one with another on the gambos of imagination between their legs; eat they do and sleep, game, laugh, and lie down, as beauties ought to do; there's all" (I.ii). A few lines earlier he has referred to their attendant, Morosa, as "an old rotten coddled mungrel, parcel-bawd, parcel-midwife." Surely Ford encourages us to take a dim view of the court to which Livio is sending Castamela.

Spadone's most important function concerns Octavio. In the first two acts, we are led to believe that both Spadone and Octavio are impotent. We have little doubt of Spadone's incapacity, for he vividly describes it and also reacts furiously to Nitido's teasing; but we are not so sure about Octavio: Is he really disabled, or is his "Bower" a harem? Indeed, the question of his manhood is not answered even in the final scene; but, since he is at that time revealed as a benevolent uncle, his physical condition is no longer crucial to the story. Until the fifth act, however, our main suspicion dwells upon the marquis. We worry not only that he may be a whole man but also that, if he is not, he is nevertheless a lecherous sensualist, an accusation Castamela makes at the end of Act III. That we have the latter "unchaste fancy" is due largely to Spadone. Because both he and Octavio are (so we are told) impotent, we cannot help associating them; consequently, as Spadone continually expresses lewdness, we tend to attribute the same attitude to the more reserved Octavio. The marquis in Act III merely asks Castamela "to be pleasant/ In practice of outward senses only," and we at once wonder what gross thoughts are racing through the mind of this second sensualist.

Ford uses similar manipulation in handling the main story of Troylo, Livio, Castamela, and Romanello; and at times his characters seem insufficiently or illogically motivated. In the play's opening lines, Troylo arouses our suspicions when, in urging Livio to accept preferment for himself and his sister, he cites—hardly a reassuring argument—the man who became grand collector at Leghorn because he "led the prince unto his wife's

chaste bed,/ And stood himself by in his night-gown, fearing/
The jest might be discover'd." Later (I.iii) Livio's initial distrust
has changed (we are never told why) to confidence, as he all
but pushes the hesitant Castamela into a court-bound coach. In
the second act, when Livio unexplainedly shifts back to anxiety,
Troylo calms him—though not us—by telling of Octavio's infirmity (II.ii). Later in the same scene, Morosa similarly alleviates
Castamela's fears. Here, probably more than anywhere else in
The Fancies, Ford plays unfairly: Morosa's language is so
pruriently suggestive—for example, "He will not press beyond
his bounds;/ He will but chat and toy, and feel your—"—that
her employer Octavio necessarily becomes suspect; Clarella's
subsequent explanation that Morosa "will prate sometimes
oddly;/ However, means but sport" (V.ii) strikes the reader
as a rather lame excuse for the earlier bawdlike role.

In Act III Ford, in order to set up his unexpected denouement
of the Troylo-Castamela match, divorces our sympathies from
her suitor, Romanello. Earlier (I.iii), the playwright cleverly has
had Castamela reject him before she is invited to court, thereby
absolving her, in our minds, of any selfishness. Now Romanello,
expecting the worst, goes to the palace disguised as a malcontent, unaware that Troylo has lured him thither. In this role,
simply by railing against womankind and by conversing with the
coarse Spadone and Morosa, he impresses us unfavorably. As the
act draws to a close, Castamela chastises Octavio as a sensualist,
but she also consents to be his guest.

In the first scene of Act IV, Livio again has strangely altered
his views; he once more worries about his sister, who now is
puzzlingly gay, even flippant. He gradually becomes furious,
calls her "strumpet," and would hasten her marriage to Romanello. Upon his exit, Troylo enters, and Castamela says to him:
"You have been counsellor/ To a strange dialogue." We doubtless sense some sort of clue here, yet certainly cannot be expected
to foresee their eventual marriage; throughout *The Fancies,*
Ford's portrayal of their relationship is sketchy, almost non-
existent. In the next scene, Livio visits Romanello to propose
the marriage; but Romanello scornfully rejects the offer and
thereby falls into Troylo's trap—though we, the benighted au-

dience, do not as yet know that one has been set. Perhaps
Romanello, and we, should have been less suspicious; for, after
all, his sister Flavia has just vindicated her honor to him. In
The Fancies, however, there is so much smoke that fires are
difficult to discern.

Act V dispels our confusion, though not before Livio (V.i)
has angrily expressed to Troylo the worst doubts of himself and
Romanello:

> Ask Romanello; he hath, without leave,
> Survey'd your Bowers of Fancies, hath discover'd
> The mystery of those pure nuns, those chaste ones,
> Untouch'd, forsooth! the holy academy!
> Hath found a mother's daughter there of mine too.

Livio challenges Troylo to a duel, but the latter persuades him
that a satisfactory explanation will be given before the day is
over. Next, we learn part of the truth (V.ii) as the three Fancies
tell Castamela that Octavio is their uncle and has taken care of
them since they were orphaned in childhood. Our fears of the
marquis's villainy having been eliminated, Ford no longer needs
Spadone's services as an indirect contaminator, so he has the
scabrous servant confess to Secco his imposture as a eunuch.

In the final scene, we learn the rest of the truth, but only after
Romanello, who as yet knows none of it, has been maneuvered
into disclaiming Castamela. When Octavio asks if he still is a
suitor, Romanello says to her:

> By no means, fair one;
> Enjoy your life of greatness. Sure, the spring
> Is past, the BOWER OF FANCIES is quite wither'd,
> And offer'd like a lottery to be drawn. (V.iii)

At this point Troylo asks Castamela to be his wife, and she
accepts him. When Romanello protests that he has been
"cozen'd," the marquis corrects him:

> You are not, Romanello: we examin'd
> On what conditions your affections fix'd,
> And found them merely courtship; but my nephew

> Lov'd with a faith resolv'd, and us'd his policy
> To draw the lady into this society,
> More freely to discover his sincerity.

Although surprised by Troylo's stratagem, we share Octavio's
lack of sympathy, for the playwright has already alienated us
from Romanello. Thus the drama ends quite contrary to our
earlier expectations. We must confess to ourselves that whereas
Octavio's three wards are eminently chaste and noble, our own
fancies—not to mention those of Livio, Romanello, Castamela,
Camillo, Vespucci, Secco, and Spadone—certainly have not been.

II   The Lady's Trial

In *The Lady's Trial*, Ford again provides a happy conclusion
to a story that initially seems destined for bloody revenge; but
his procedure is different. Instead of utilizing a surprise ending,
he portrays his two main characters, Auria and Spinella, as a husband and wife whose love and reason enable them to avoid
tragedy despite great provocation. *The Lady's Trial*, culminating
in discussion rather than violence, is not one of Ford's more
colorful plays. We could argue, nevertheless, that Ford deliberately discards in it the convention of murderous revenge in
order to show two mature people handling most capably a threat
to their marriage.

Because of financial problems, Auria, a Genoese noble and
soldier, offers his military services to the Duke of Florence, who
is fighting the Turks. Bidding farewell to his young and beautiful wife, Spinella, he advises her to protect her reputation. Auria
in turn is warned by his best friend, Aurelio, that he is leaving
an innocent wife with "no shelter for her honor." While Auria
is away, Aurelio believes his worst fears are realized, for he
discovers Spinella in a compromising situation, banqueting with
Adurni, a young lord, in the latter's chamber. Actually Spinella
is guiltless, having spurned her host's advances.

Meanwhile, Adurni's former mistress, Levidolche, repents of
her wanton ways; when her deserted husband, Benatzi, appears
disguised as a malcontent soldier, she recognizes him but does
not tell him so; and she agrees to marry him if he will slay
Adurni for her. At the same time, two of Adurni's attendants,

Futelli and Piero, play a trick on Amoretta, a young lady who aspires to position and wealth: they persuade both Guzman ("a braggadoccio Spaniard") and Fulgoso ("an upstart gallant") to woo her as rich lords.

After a short time, Auria returns victorious from the wars and is honored by Genoa with both money and the governorship of Corsica. His wife, however, has disappeared, having been upset by Aurelio's suspicion of her integrity. Aurelio urges Auria to seek revenge for the banquet-chamber incident, but the husband argues for his wife's innocence and charges his friend with slander and "giddy zeal." After the two have drawn their weapons, Auria realizes their folly and they are reconciled, Aurelio deferring to Auria's point of view. Then Adurni, the unsuccessful seducer, poses a new problem when he visits Auria to inform him that although he had most dishonorable intentions concerning the virtuous Spinella, he has now repented of his sinfulness and hence deserves no punishment; Auria, confronted with this unexpected excuse, temporizes.

In the play's final scene, Spinella, having been told of Auria's defense of her reputation, returns from the house of her cousin, Malfato, only to be put on "trial" by her husband. Ably defending herself, she charges Aurelio with "traducing spotless honour," but is overwhelmed when her husband demands satisfaction from Adurni. Auria, however, has simply been testing her virtue: his challenge of Adurni was pretense, for he has already arranged a marriage between the lord and Spinella's sister, Castanna. Other characters also find happiness: Benatzi and Levidolche are reunited, while Amoretta, having acquired some common sense, is to marry Futelli even though he is "not the richest/ I' th' parish."

Ford's major point in *The Lady's Trial* is that love should be perceptive enough to withstand misleading appearances; two secondary ones are that repentance should be accepted and that in marriage love is more important than wealth. Each of these three themes appears in the central plot as well as in one or both of the play's two subplots. In the main plot, danger to Spinella is foreshadowed in the play's opening lines in which Futelli and Piero describe Auria as leaving his young wife "to buffet/ Land pirates here at home." Auria himself raises the

possibility of slandered reputation when he kindly advises
Spinella to conduct herself with discretion, and Aurelio criticizes
him for marrying a beautiful but dowerless woman and then
putting her "to the trial of her wits" (I.i). In Act II, we learn
that Spinella has not entirely heeded her absent husband's
counsel; for Fulgoso has seen her lose some money at the gam-
bling table (II.i). She errs more disastrously in visiting Adurni
(II.i), though accompanied by Castanna and Amoretta. She
soon is left alone when Futelli and Piero escort the other two
women into a picture gallery, and she next appears (II.iv)
with Adurni in his banquet chamber as erotic lyrics are sung
offstage. When Adurni tries to seduce her, she denounces him;
but then Aurelio, forcing open the door, rebukes her as a "vow-
breaking wanton." Adurni, whom Ford now quickly converts
from a libertine to a gallant defender of maligned innocence,
reassures her, "I will stand champion for your honour," but
Spinella departs alone and says, "I need no followers now:
let me appear/ Or mine own lawyer, or in open court."

Auria, having returned to Genoa a military hero, worries about
his missing wife: "for't had been pity she should ever/ Have
felt so much extremity" (III.iii). Aurelio, his indignant friend,
replies: "This is not/ Patience requir'd in wrongs of such vile
nature:/ You pity her; think rather on revenge." But Auria
strongly disagrees:

> Revenge! for what, uncharitable friend?
> On whom? let's speak a little, pray, with reason.
> You found Spinella in Adurni's house;
> 'Tis like he gave her welcome—very likely;
> Her sister and another with her; so!
> Invited, nobly done; but he with her
> Privately chamber'd:—he deserves no wife
> Of worthy quality who dares not trust
> Her virtue in the proofs of any danger. (III.iii)

In this passage, Ford abandons the typical pattern of domestic
tragedy. In *Love's Sacrifice* D'Avolos, like Iago, incites a husband to murder his wife; but in *The Lady's Trial* Auria's clear-
headed compassion prevails and revenge is not sought.

In Act IV Spinella, at the house of her cousin, Malfato,

displays similar wisdom not only by ignoring the latter's declaration of love but by discouraging his championing of her reputation; then Castanna enters with the welcome news that Auria, far from being angry, "only grieves/ At his soul's love, Spinella's, causeless absence" (IV.i). Later in the same act, Ford departs even further from the revenge stereotype when Adurni confesses to Auria that he intended to seduce Spinella in the banquet chamber and when, before the husband's rising wrath can erupt as physical violence, he adds, "I've robb'd you/ Of rigour, Auria, by my strict self-penance" (IV.ii). Auria, in words describing the novel procedure of Ford as well as of Adurni, replies, "Sure, Italians hardly/ Admit dispute in questions of this nature;/ The trick is new." Adurni persists, "I find my absolution/By vows of change from all ignoble practise," and the act ends indecisively with Auria walking apart and musing, "That's the way;/ It smooths all rubs."

When Spinella returns to her husband (V.ii), Auria, instead of greeting her with open arms, asks her to "stand the trial." She is surprised, and Malfato is furious. She shows her mettle, however, by eloquently charging Aurelio with "traducing spotless honour." Auria then presses her: he cites their difference in age and their lack of wealth, but argues that, since they married for love, "the breach in such a case appears/ Unpardonable." To this statement, which could be construed as Auria's testing of her love, Spinella replies that, while sharing his view of their marriage, she objects to a "charge of disloyalty . . . Without a ground or witness." At this point Malfato seeks some sort of action: if Spinella has "lewdly rang'd," her husband should exact vengeance; if she is innocent, then he, Malfato, will avenge the slander. Immediately Adurni enters and says that he desired to seduce Spinella; Auria pretends to be outraged, and Spinella, overcome by her husband's apparent lack of trust, collapses.

Auria at once reassures her that all is well, that he has found her virtue "perfect,/ Pure and unflaw'd"; he also explains that he has arranged a marriage between her sister and Adurni, whereupon even the ever suspicious Aurelio is satisfied: "This marriage frees/ Each circumstance of jealousy." Auria then states that this match has accounted for his previous inaction in regard to Adurni:

> Why else have I so long with tameness nourish'd
> Report of wrongs, but that I fix'd on issue
> Of my desires? Italians use not dalliance,
> But execution.

And Spinella's trial ends, not with revenge, but with reconciliation.

The Levidolche subplot, though sometimes censured as implausible, is quite relevant to the drama. At first obviously a loose woman, Levidolche soon renounces, in a soliloquy, her illicit relationships with Adurni and Malfato (II.ii). Not until much later is she judged rightly by them. Nor does her uncle Martino readily believe in her reformation; when she informs him (V.i) that she has married the poorly clad Parado (really Benatzi in disguise), Martino takes one look at her partner and concludes that "Parado" is a thief and his niece a whore. By rejoining her husband despite his poverty, Levidolche becomes a loyal wife. And the couple's financial difficulties are solved (V.ii) when Spinella, Castanna, and Adurni—who now, along with Malfato and Martino, accepts Levidolche's conversion— bestow money upon them.

Similarities to the Auria-Spinella story are several. Like Auria, Benatzi is a soldier whose lack of wealth does not diminish his wife's love. Like Spinella, Levidolche is a victim of slander, though the latter's previous adultery and secret repentance make Martino's denunciations of her more defensible than those of Aurelio against Spinella. Another parallel is that between Levidolche and Adurni, both of whom repent earlier indiscretions; furthermore, Levidolche's contrition, by preceding Adurni's, makes us more receptive to the lord's unexpected request for Auria's pardon. A significant difference between the two married couples—Auria and Spinella, Benatzi and Levidolche—lies in their attitudes toward revenge. Levidolche urges Benatzi to slay Adurni and Malfato (III.iv), and Benatzi later rushes in with drawn sword (V.ii). On the other hand, Auria rejects Aurelio's demand for violence (III.iii), and Spinella dissaudes her cousin, Malfato, from taking action (IV.i).

The other subplot, which presents Amoretta, Guzman, and Fulgoso, is thematically related to the rest of the drama in

several ways. First of all, Amoretta's ludicrous desire for any
rich nobleman contrasts with the unselfish loves of Spinella and
Levidolche for their husbands, and her eventual match with
the unwealthy and untitled Futelli shows her recognition of folly.
Besides condemning materialism, the Amoretta subplot also
illustrates mistaking appearance for reality, exemplified in the
main story by Aurelio's suspicions of Spinella and in the other
subplot by Martino's erroneous estimates of Levidolche and
Benatzi. For Amoretta, during most of the play, believes that
the braggart Guzman and the upstart Fulgoso are opulent lords
and mighty warriors. Here another contrast becomes obvious—
that between the pair of cowardly pretenders and the two real
soldiers, Auria and Benatzi.

Such relevance of theme and characterization notwithstanding,
the subplot is ineffectual. What are intended to be comical
verbal pyrotechnics of Guzman, who bombastically declaims
about costly clothes, bloody battles, Petrarchan mistress, and
Gargantuan genealogy, seem to misfire, even when juxtaposed to
the low cant of Fulgoso. An instance is Guzman's comment on
Fulgoso's use of "wench" to describe Amoretta:

> Wench said ye? most mechanically, faugh!
> Wench is your trull, your blowse, your dowdy, but,
> Sir brother, he who names my queen of love
> Without his bonnet vail'd, or saying grace,
> As at some paranymphal feast, is rude,
> Nor vers'd in literature. Dame Amoretta,
> Lo, I am sworn thy champion! (III.i)

To this hubbub, Ford adds the even shriller voice of Benatzi,
who, approaching the two pretenders as a malcontent, spews
forth satire: "Cutthroats by the score abroad, come home, and
rot in fripperies. Brave man at arms, go turn pander, do; stalk
for a mess of warm broth—damnable! honourable cuts are but
badges for a fool to vaunt; the raw-ribb'd apothecary poisons
cum privilegio, and is paid. O, the commonwealth of beasts is
most politicly ordered!" (III.i). The language of the three characters is colorful (and Amoretta's lisp should not be forgotten);
but, on the whole, its style, diction, and tone pull against rather
than with the rest of the drama. Because the speech of the

play."[1] Ford is also mentioned briefly by Edward Phillips (1675), William Winstanley (1687), and Gerald Langbaine (1688).[2] In the eighteenth century two of his plays were performed: *Perkin Warbeck* in 1745 and *The Lover's Melancholy* in 1748. The only commentary of this era is provided by David Baker, who in his *Biographia Dramatica* (1782) praises both *The Lover's Melancholy* and *'Tis Pity;* but he censures "the morals" of the latter.[3]

Lamb's criticism (1808), while rather short, was influential. His enthusiasm for the playwright in *Specimens of English Dramatic Poets* aroused public interest and largely accounted for Henry Weber's 1811 edition of Ford; it also drew eventual rebuttal from Hazlitt and others. Not only does Lamb admire Calantha's death in *The Broken Heart,* which carries him "in imagination to Calvary and the Cross," [4] but he also defends *'Tis Pity:* "There is a grandeur of the soul above mountains, seas and the elements. Even in the poor perverted reason of Giovanni and Annabella . . . we discern traces of that fiery particle which shows hints of an improveable greatness in the lowest descents and degradations of our nature."[5] Hazlitt (1820), however, finds in Ford nothing of merit.[6] The last scene of *The Broken Heart,* extolled by Lamb, he calls "extravagant"; in *'Tis Pity* he sees the dramatist as "playing with edged tools, and knowing the use of poisoned weapons"; Ford's style is characterized by "an artificial elaborateness"; and his dramas, "where they have not the sting of illicit passion, . . . are quite pointless, and seem painted on gauze, or spun of cobwebs."[7]

Later in the century the two-sided criticism of Ford is continued by Lowell (1845), Swinburne (1875), Havelock Ellis (1888), Taine (1864), and George Saintsbury (1896). Ellis and Taine admire; Lowell and Saintsbury are unsympathetic; and Swinburne lies somewhere between, though closer to the former pair. Lowell asserts that Ford's characters are sentimental because they defy the inevitable—death: "What one dies for, not his dying, glorifies him." And the breaking of Calantha's heart strikes him as "too palpable and anatomical an event."[8] Swinburne, though qualifying his praise, is more favorable:[9] most noticeable in Ford's poetry is "the passionless reason and equable tone of style with which in his greatest works he treats of the deepest and most fiery passions." Yet Ford's language lacks "pure imagination," and the critic sometimes finds "a certain hardness of tone peculiar to him." Ford's greatest characterization, says Swinburne, is that of Giovanni: "Here the poet has put forth all his strength; the figure of his protagonist stands out complete and clear." [10]

Ellis and Taine share Swinburne's admiration for *'Tis Pity*. In it, says Ellis, "Ford touched the highest point he ever reached." Speaking of all the plays, he calls the dramatist "the most modern of the tribe to whom he belonged. . . . He was an analyst; he strained the limits of his art to the utmost; he foreboded new ways of expression."[11] Taine states that in *'Tis Pity* Ford has reached the limits of tragedy, writing "sincere melodrama" and that there is no scene more pure and touching than that of Penthea's death in *The Broken Heart*.[12] Saintsbury admits the power of *'Tis Pity*—"the sheer effects of passion . . . have never been so rendered in English except in *Romeo and Juliet* and *Antony and Cleopatra*"—but brands Fordian drama with "decadence,"[13] a charge soon repeated by Felix Schelling, Ashley Thorndike, and Sherman (all three writing in 1908), although Sherman also views Ford, "in rebellion against . . . society," as creator of "the problem play." [14]

II *Twentieth-Century Views*

In 1932, Eliot offered a series of provocative opinions, most of them unfavorable to the playwright:[15] Ford's poetry lacks "symbolic value" and "inner significance"; *'Tis Pity* is "meaningless" and without "emotional depth"; and Giovanni is "merely selfish and self-willed, of a temperament to want a thing the more because it is forbidden." Eliot's criticism has not been generally accepted, and his estimate of *'Tis Pity* has been strongly challenged by Sargeaunt and Davril. Several years later two other important works appeared: Sargeaunt's *John Ford* (1935) and Ellis-Fermor's *The Jacobean Drama* (1936). Sargeaunt's book-length study of Ford presents new biographical information and also has much to say about his earlier, nondramatic writings as well as about his possible authorship of *The Queen*.[16] Ellis-Fermor, in her chapter on Ford, sees him as Middleton's successor in the "close analysis of hitherto disregarded or less fully examined movements of the mind." The touchstone of his art is its "firm elasticity," its "rapidity of inner realization and stillness of outward demeanor simultaneously indicated." [17]

In the past thirty years there have been six books on Ford: Ewing's *Burtonian Melancholy in the Plays of John Ford* (1940), Sensabaugh's *The Tragic Muse of John Ford* (1944), Davril's *Le Drame de John Ford* (1954), Oliver's *The Problem of John Ford* (1955), Leech's *John Ford and the Drama of His Time* (1957), and Mark Stavig's *John Ford and the Traditional Moral Order* (1968). Ewing's work is, in his own words, "a detailed study of the indebtedness of John Ford's plays to Robert Burton's *Anatomy of Melancholy*"; [18] he finds Burtonian influence in the characterization of Giovanni, Ithocles, Bassanes, Octavio, and others. Sensabaugh, who discusses Fordian tragedy in terms of "scientific determinism" and "unbridled individualism," associates the determinism with Burton's psychology, and the individualism with Neoplatonism, especially that at the court of Henrietta Maria, wife of Charles I; Sensabaugh argues for "the modernity of Ford's tragic muse." [19]

Davril's book contains in its five hundred and fifty-four pages not only considerable information about sources and analogues but discerning analyses of Ford's themes, characterization, and language. Concerning language, for instance, Davril explains that an unusually high percentage of Ford's nouns are polysyllabic, Latinate, and abstract and that the uncommonly numerous prepositional phrases beginning with *of* help to create a slow cadence, particularly when linking two of the aforementioned nouns. [20] Oliver notes Ford's "concentration on states of mind" and finds him a "constant experimenter" who, in some of his techniques, anticipates the modern novel. Oliver also is knowledgeable and judicious about the probabilities both of Ford's authorship of *The Golden Mean* and *Christ's Bloody Sweat* and of his collaboration with other dramatists. [21]

Leech sees as central in Ford's dramas an "aristocratic code of endurance," which he thinks "a product of the 'private' theatres." [22] Leech also finds a relationship between the plays and the nondramatic works, which exalt "the exceptional human being who in the depth of adversity is above [pity]," and he argues that Ford's crude comic figures are not a blemish but created as foils to the nobler characters.[23] Most recently, Stavig contends that the playwright is neither a hothouse decadent nor a social rebel but a staunch supporter of the traditional moral order; that, for example, Ford ridicules Giovanni and his other tragic protagonists by satirizing them as fools.[24] Stavig and Sensabaugh mark the two poles of twentieth-century commentary, the former arguing the dramatist's conservatism, the latter his "unbridled individualism." Most of the current critics, including myself, place Ford midway between these two extremes, finding him both compassionate and condemnatory toward his characters.

III *Conclusion*

What is one to say about Fordian criticism and, finally, about the plays themselves? Of the myriad commentaries, several of the more prevalent should be challenged. The word *terminal* adequately describes one such viewpoint, which sees Ford mainly as a playwright active shortly before the closing of the theaters in 1642 by a Puritan Parliament hostile to drama and worried about impending civil war. Because many histories of Elizabethan drama stop at this date, Ford, as well as Massinger and Shirley, is sometimes victimized by scholars who have decided a priori on a rise-and-fall pattern for English drama between 1558 and 1642; we are almost led to believe that performances would have sputtered to a halt if there had been no hostile Puritans. Another favorite epithet for Ford is *decadent*. As with *terminal*, this adjective has frequently resulted from a chronological sweep that fails to distinguish among individual Jacobean and Caroline dramatists, or among different plays by the same author. For example, Fletcher is, to me, more decadent than Ford; and *The Fancies* is more decadent than *The Broken Heart*. A third term, *aristocratic*, is used by those who, overlooking the outspoken middle-class personae in *'Tis Pity* and *Love's Sacrifice*, discover the quintessence of Ford in the composedly suffering nobles of *The Broken Heart*, *Perkin Warbeck*, *The Lover's Melancholy*, and *The Queen*. Often accompanying *aristocratic* is *amateur*, which usually implies a gentleman neither

financially dependent upon the theater nor particularly concerned with the tricks of the trade.

These views vary, of course, according to their different purposes and premises. If a scholar is writing a history of Elizabethan drama, he can spend no more than a few pages—at the
most, a chapter—on a single playwright, whom he must isolate
from the rest by means of any unique traits available. This
procedure, though understandable, accounts for the unmerited
downgrading of *'Tis Pity* in much twentieth-century criticism,
which, seeking a distinctive Fordian note, must prefer *The
Broken Heart,* which is, after all, less reminiscent of Shakespeare and his contemporaries. For a survey of many writers,
such an approach may be necessary; but, for a book devoted
entirely to one dramatist who wrote only seven extant unaided
plays (eight, if *The Queen* be included) in an unknown sequence, a more inductive method seems wiser. Thus, instead of
initially assuming that Ford is decadent or that his literary career
should culminate in or be typified by one play, I have examined
each drama primarily in terms of itself. One result has been a
closer look than heretofore at *The Lover's Melancholy* and
Love's Sacrifice.

Critics, in general agreement as to the distinguishing traits
of Ford's style, have pointed to a slow and regular cadence, a
restrained rendering of strong emotion, a lack of copiousness, and
abstraction. These characteristics are undeniably Ford's and
must be acknowledged vital to his dramatic effectiveness. At the
same time, they do not tell the whole story; for, in the first
place, a subdued style is prominent in only three plays (*The
Broken Heart, The Lover's Melancholy,* and *Perkin Warbeck*);
and, even in them, with the exception of Palador, this style is
confined to women. The language of *'Tis Pity* and *Love's Sacrifice* is, if anything, violent; when Annabella and Bianca respond
to their accusing husbands, they sound more like the brazen
Vittoria Corombona of Webster's *The White Devil* than like
Ford's Penthea, Eroclea, and Katherine Gordon. In addition, the
more quiet plays are at times clamorous; for muted voices are
punctuated or balanced by loud ones: Palador's lethargy alter-
nates with Meleander's frenzy; Penthea's silence is complemented
by Bassanes's shrillness; and Katherine's stoical resignation is

offset by Warbeck's unflagging eloquence (his contempt for Simnel and defiance of Henry VII, for instance) as well as by Huntley's blazing resentment. In most of his dramas, Ford achieves additional antiphony by means of boisterous comical personae and also by juxtaposing the decorous language of courtly love with Juvenalian tirades against sensuality.

In the second place, Ford's imagery, while not copious, often is so sustained as to enhance characterization and theme. The ephemeral success of Ithocles is underlined by plummeting dove, fireworks, mushroom, Phaeton, and Ixion; Bassanes's coarseness is continually depicted by reference to animals. Banquet and heart imagery abounds in both *'Tis Pity* and *The Broken Heart*. In *'Tis Pity*, this language portrays both metaphorically and literally the theme of lust and death; in *The Broken Heart*, it similarly depicts the theme of abstinence and death.

But, aside from criticizing the critics, what can one add to Fordian scholarship? Probably the chief contribution of the present book is its exposition of Ford's knowledgeable dramaturgy. We have seen, for example, how he presents in *The Lover's Melancholy* the separate cures of Palador and Meleander in six suspenseful and interwoven scenes; how in *Perkin Warbeck* he achieves a contrast in kingship by alternate scenes in England and Scotland and manages to make Warbeck both ineffectual and admirable; how in *Love's Sacrifice* he establishes, by means of Ferentes and other devices, a Neoplatonic code for tragedy; and how in *The Fancies Chaste and Noble*, his most contrived play, he cleverly handles both his personae and his audience. Occasionally, his structures are poorly joined: in four plays a subplot featuring a proud lady scorned seems irrelevant to the main story; so do some of his humorous characters. But he is usually successful, and always interested, in arranging his material.

If we look for some unifying principles in Ford's plays, we find in most of them, first of all, what might be called the threatened marriage, a pattern dominating four works and appearing in two others. The main plot of *'Tis Pity*, *Love's Sacrifice*, *The Lady's Trial*, and *The Queen* consists of a domestic situation in which the wife has a lover, actual or alleged, and in which the husband has a friend who discovers, or claims to have discovered, the lover and tries to arouse the husband to vengeance. In *'Tis Pity*, Vasques learns from the nurse that Giovanni is responsible for Annabella's pregnancy and goads Soranzo to an Italianate revenge; in *Love's Sacrifice*, D'Avolos, having seen Fernando kneel before Bianca, mistakenly concludes they are guilty of adultery and rouses the duke to homicidal fury; in *The Lady's Trial*, Aurelio finds Spinella and Adurni in the banquet chamber and demands that Auria seek satisfaction; and, in *The Queen*, Alphonso is convinced by Muretto that the queen and Petruchio are secret lovers.

Although these four plays have many significant differences, their similarity in plot argues that Ford has a particular context in which he likes to work. This pattern also appears, though to a lesser extent, in *Perkin Warbeck* and *The Broken Heart*. In the former, the unfortunate suitor Daliell (a character not to be found in any of Ford's chronicle sources) seems a potential challenge to the marriage of Warbeck and Katherine until he accedes completely to James's matchmaking. As for *The Broken Heart*, Ford begins with his favorite situation, then modifies it. In the first two acts, Orgilus, secretly meeting Bassanes's wife, Penthea, and claiming her love, sets the stage for a typical Fordian triangle. Penthea rejects Orgilus, however, and thereby begins a different set of relationships. A suspicious husband is still there, but the informing confidant is supplanted by Bassanes's insane jealousy, which directs his wrath not toward Penthea's lover but toward her brother.

Ford also frequently demonstrates a unique manner of handling both revenge and love and of combining them. Revenge, prominent in at least four of his plays, he surely inherits from Elizabethan drama; it appears in none of his earlier works, either the nondramatic ones or the extant collaborations with Dekker. Yet Ford differs from earlier playwrights in that he subordinates revenge. Such works as Kyd's *The Spanish Tragedy*, Shakespeare's *Titus Andronicus*, Cyril Tourneur's (or Middleton's) *The Revenger's Tragedy*, and Webster's *The Duchess of Malfi*, to name only a few, are dominated by blood lust and, once the victim or victims have been trapped, by a cat-and-mouse toying that prolongs suspense; but Ford's emphasis lies elsewhere. Even in *'Tis Pity*, his bloodiest tragedy, the several murders resulting from vengeance are witnessed by a surprised rather than expectant audience: the innocent Bergetto is mistaken by his assassin for Soranzo; Hippolita has already drunk her own poison before we learn, along with her, of Vasques's trickery; and our anticipation that the cuckolded Soranzo will slay the incestuous Giovanni and Annabella while they are making love in her chamber is suddenly overwhelmed by the appearance of Giovanni with his sister's heart on his dagger.

Typical Elizabethan vengeance undergoes equally drastic alteration in some of Ford's other plays. *The Broken Heart* begins with Orgilus as the familiar revenger, but his prominence fades in Act III and most of Act IV, which focus on Penthea's grief and on the romance of Ithocles and Calantha. At the end of Act IV, immediately after Penthea's quiet death, Orgilus unexpectedly resumes his role of avenger when he traps Ithocles in the mechanical chair and murders him. This explosive action, however, is soon assimilated by the drama's dominant tone of restraint; Orgilus formally bleeds himself to death with a discipline and decorum matching that of Calantha, who wills to die of a broken heart. Whereas revenge gives way to tone in *The Broken Heart*, it yields to theme in *Love's Sacrifice* and *The Lady's Trial*. In the former work, conventional domestic tragedy would point toward the duke's exacting vengeance on his wife (Bianca) and her lover (Fernando); the duke does kill Bianca in Act V, but here the Fordian twist—the play's unusual moral code—makes her punishment undeserved and hence results in the remorseful husband's suicide. In *The Lady's Trial*, Ford goes so far as to convert incipient revenge into peaceful reconciliation. Although a wife is discovered in a compromising situation, her husband, despite goadings from his best friend, insists on her fidelity; and, even when her would-be seducer admits his adulterous intentions, there is no bloodshed.

Ford's treatment of revenge is best explained by its relationship to what seems the ultimate concern of most of his plays: love between man and woman. Although love between brother and sister and between father and daughter is sometimes depicted, romantic love always is central. Furthermore, with Ford, this love is extremely intense; his characters willingly die for it.

No one has yet observed, however, that to achieve such an effect Ford relies heavily upon revenge. Since in his plays intensity of hatred is regularly surpassed by intensity of love, the more virulent he makes the former, the more powerful becomes the latter. The two clearest examples of this technique occur in *'Tis Pity* and *Love's Sacrifice*. In *'Tis Pity*, the fury of a vengeful husband is outdone, first, by a flaunting wife and, later, by her incestuous lover, who berates and then kills the husband; in *Love's Sacrifice*, the aroused husband functions similarly: how strong must be the love between Bianca and Fernando since each in turn makes the duke's anger pale in comparison! Ford also subordinates revenge to love by making the second more ceremonial. In earlier plays of lust and blood, death-defying vows are uttered by avengers, not by lovers. So swear Shakespeare's Titus Andronicus and his brother Marcus, and Othello and Iago. In Ford's dramas, the lovers make the prominent gestures, kneel, hold hands, and vow. This ritual is performed in all of the tragedies: by Giovanni and Annabella, by Fernando and Bianca, by Orgilus and Penthea (not to mention the concluding marriage-in-death of Ithocles and Calantha), and by Warbeck and Katherine, when the wife kneels by her husband in the stocks to vow her present and future love. And, in all of these scenes, hyperbolic language approaching deification of the loved one adds to the intensity.

Finally, something should be said concerning Ford's tragic protagonists. Giovanni, Ithocles, Fernando, and Warbeck are all handsome and aggressive young men who, endeavoring to realize their aspirations, die with courage and defiance. Thus Ford's tragedies are dynamic, not static; some of his women may be submissive, but his men are not. Ford exalts resolution as well as love, and we should not forget that he earlier wrote both *The Golden Mean* and *Honour Triumphant*. At the same time, Lowell's objection comes to mind: is not what a man dies for more important than how he dies? In this sense, Giovanni and Warbeck are most vulnerable, for their respective aims of incest and usurpation challenge the very basis of society; the playwright puts us in the ambivalent position of admiring an attractive champion of an unacceptable cause. Yet, in Ford's hands, paradox becomes provocative and esthetically satisfying; and we wonder, indeed, if it does not truly describe life itself.

Notes and References

Chapter One

1. Gerald E. Bentley, *The Jacobean and Caroline Stage* (Oxford, 1941–56), III, 437.
2. According to T. J. King, many of the plays staged at the Phoenix, including Ford's *'Tis Pity She's a Whore* and *Love's Sacrifice*, utilized a "discovery space" and "an acting area above" where "characters comment on, or converse with, characters below." See "Staging of Plays at the Phoenix in Drury Lane, 1617–42," *Theatre Notebook*, XIX (Spring, 1965), 146–66.
3. M. Joan Sargeaunt, *John Ford* (Oxford, 1935), p. 212, n. 9. The information below concerning Ford's stay at the Middle Temple comes from Sargeaunt's first chapter, "Ford's Early Life and Writings," pp. 1–16.
4. Bentley, *The Jacobean and Caroline Stage*, III, 434.
5. *Ibid.*, pp. 434–35.

Chapter Two

1. Quotations from *Fame's Memorial* come from *The Works of John Ford*, William Gifford and Alexander Dyce, eds. (London, 1895).
2. *Dictionary of National Biography* (New York, 1908), II, 705.
3. Bertram Lloyd, "An Inedited MS. of Ford's *Fames Memoriall*," *Review of English Studies*, I (January, 1925), 94.
4. Stuart P. Sherman, "Stella and *The Broken Heart*," *PMLA*, XIV (1909), 274–85.
5. See the *Dictionary of National Biography*, II, 702–5.
6. Quotations from *Honour Triumphant* come from the Gifford and Dyce edition.
7. Clifford Leech, *John Ford and the Drama of his Time* (London, 1957), p. 21.
8. Quotations from *Christ's Bloody Sweat* come from the first edition (London, 1613).
9. Leech, *John Ford and the Drama of His Time*, p. 22, n. 1.
10. M. Joan Sargeaunt, "Writings Ascribed to John Ford by Joseph

143

Hunter in *Chorus Vatum,*" *Review of English Studies,* X (April, 1934), 165–76.
11. *Ibid.,* pp. 173–74.
12. Harold J. Oliver, *The Problem of John Ford* (Melbourne, 1955), p. 12.
13. Robert Davril, *Le Drame de John Ford* (Paris, 1954), p. 86, n. 43.
14. Quotations from *The Golden Mean* come from the first edition (London, 1613).
15. Sargeaunt, "Writings Ascribed to John Ford by Joseph Hunter in *Chorus Vatum,*" p. 174.
16. Oliver, *The Problem of John Ford,* p. 18.
17. Davril, *Le Drame de John Ford,* pp. 89–90.
18. Quotations from *A Line of Life* come from the Gifford and Dyce edition.
19. Oliver, *The Problem of John Ford,* 18–20.

Chapter Three
1. Bentley, *The Jacobean and Caroline Stage,* III, 436.
2. In 1653, Moseley entered in the Stationers' Register and attributed to Ford *Beauty in a Trance* (lost), which had been performed by the King's company in 1630; in 1660, he did the same for *An Ill Beginning Has a Good End* (lost), *The London Merchant* (lost), and *The Royal Combat* (lost). The reliability of his listings has been questioned, however. Harbage ("Elizabethan-Restoration Palimpsest," *Modern Language Review,* XXXV [July, 1940], 297–304) claims that Ford, rather than Henry Shirley, wrote *The Spanish Duke of Lerma* (lost), which may exist in revised form as Sir Robert Howard's *The Great Favourite, or The Duke of Lerma* (1658). Two extant plays in which some have seen Ford's hand are the anonymous *The Welsh Ambassador* (1623?) and *The Fair Maid of the Inn* (licensed in 1626 as by Fletcher). For the former drama, Bertram Lloyd ("The Authorship of *The Welsh Ambassador,*" *Review of English Studies,* XXI [July, 1945], 192–201), on the basis of style, thinks Dekker the principal author and Ford the writer of two scenes. For the latter, F. L. Lucas (*The Complete Works of John Webster* [London, 1927], IV, 152), denies Fletcher's authorship and attributes the play to Webster, Massinger, and Ford.
3. Quotations from *The Witch of Edmonton* come from the Gifford and Dyce edition.
4. H. Dugdale Sykes, *Sidelights on Elizabethan Drama* (Oxford, 1924), p. 226.
5. Oliver, *The Problem of John Ford,* p. 25.
6. Quotations from *The Sun's Darling* come from the Gifford and Dyce edition.

7. See W. L. Halstead, "Dekker's 'Phaethon,'" *Notes and Queries,* CLXXV (November, 1938), 380–85.

8. Oliver, *The Problem of John Ford,* p. 40, n. 22.

9. Bentley, *The Jacobean and Caroline Stage,* III, 461.

10. Oliver, *The Problem of John Ford,* pp. 39–40.

11. H. K. Russell, "Tudor and Stuart Dramatizations of the Doctrines of Natural and Moral Philosophy," *Studies in Philology,* XXXI (January, 1934), 18–20.

12. Sykes, *Sidelights on Elizabethan Drama,* pp. 183–99.

13. Sargeaunt, *John Ford,* pp. 41–57.

14. Oliver, *The Problem of John Ford,* p. 34.

15. W. Bang (ed.), *The Queen* (Louvain, 1906), vii–ix, 41–57. Quotations from the play come from this edition.

16. See Stuart P. Sherman, "A New Play by John Ford," *Modern Language Notes,* XXIII (December, 1908), 245–49; Sykes, *Sidelights on Elizabethan Drama,* pp. 173–82; and Sargeaunt, *John Ford,* Appendix I.

17. S. Blaine Ewing, Jr., *Burtonian Melancholy in the Plays of John Ford* (Princeton, 1940), pp. 32–46, 79–87.

18. Davril, *Le Drame de John Ford,* p. 156.

19. *Ibid.,* pp. 157–58.

Chapter Four

1. Quotations from *The Lover's Melancholy* come from the Gifford and Dyce edition.

2. See No. VI in *Famiani Stradae Romani . . . Prolusiones Academicae* (1621), Crashaw's *Music's Duel* (1648), and Philip's *Fifth Pastoral* (1709).

3. Ewing, *Burtonian Melancholy in the Plays of John Ford,* pp. 5–6, 34, 37.

Chapter Five

1. Quotations from *The Broken Heart* come from the edition by Donald K. Anderson, Jr., for the Regents Renaissance Drama Series (Lincoln, Nebraska, 1968).

2. Bentley, *The Jacobean and Caroline Stage,* III, 441–42.

3. Sherman, "Stella and *The Broken Heart,*" pp. 274–85.

4. Davril, *Le Drame de John Ford,* p. 176.

5. George F. Sensabaugh, *The Tragic Muse of John Ford* (Stanford, 1944), pp. 94–173.

6. Davril, *Le Drame de John Ford,* pp. 351–52.

7. Ewing, *Burtonian Melancholy in the Plays of John Ford,* pp. 55–64.

8. William C. Hazlitt, *Lectures on the Age of Elizabeth* (London, 1884), p. 141.

9. See Gifford and Dyce edition of the play.

10. Davril, *Le Drame de John Ford,* pp. 177–78.

11. See Glenn H. Blayney, "Convention, Plot, and Structure in *The Broken Heart,*" *Modern Philology,* LVI (August, 1958), 1–9.

Chapter Six

1. Quotations from *Perkin Warbeck* come from the edition by Donald K. Anderson, Jr., for the Regents Renaissance Drama Series (Lincoln, Nebraska, 1965).

2. *Ibid.* The explanatory notes contain many such passages from Bacon and Gainsford.

3. See Donald K. Anderson, Jr., "*Richard II* and *Perkin Warbeck,*" *Shakespeare Quarterly,* XIII (Spring, 1962), 260–63.

4. See, for example, Mildred C. Struble, *A Critical Edition of Ford's Perkin Warbeck* (Seattle, 1926), pp. 30–37. Bentley disagrees with her (*The Jacobean and Caroline Stage,* III, 455).

5. See Donald K. Anderson, Jr., "The Date and Handwriting of a Manuscript Copy of Ford's *Perkin Warbeck,*" *Notes and Queries,* X (September, 1963), 340–41.

6. This association is made by William Slatyer in *The History of Great Britaine* (1621), p. iii; by Thomas Gainsford in *The Vision and Discourse of Henry the Seventh* (1610), pp. 8 and 65; and by Sir John Beaumont (1587–1627) in his poem *Bosworth Field.*

7. See Lawrence Babb, "Abnormal Psychology in John Ford's *Perkin Warbeck,*" *Modern Language Notes,* LI (1936), 234–37.

8. See John J. O'Connor, "A Lost Play of Perkin Warbeck," *Modern Language Notes,* LXX (1955), 566. O'Connor cites the following passage in Thomas Gainsford's *True History of the Earl of Tyrone* (1619), p. 4: "How Perkin Warbeck . . . went forward . . . against the house of *Lancaster,* our stages of *London,* haue instructed those which cannot read."

9. See Donald K. Anderson, Jr., "Kingship in Ford's *Perkin Warbeck,*" *ELH,* XXVII (September, 1960), 177–93.

10. *The Works of Francis Bacon,* James Spedding, Robert L. Ellis, and Douglas D. Heath, eds. (Boston, 1857–64), XI, 357–58, 363–64.

11. *The True and Wonderful History of Perkin Warbeck* (appendix to Struble's edition of Ford's *Perkin Warbeck*), p. 196.

12. Bacon, *Works,* XI, 289.

13. Gainsford, *The True and Wonderful History of Perkin Warbeck,* pp. 191–93.

14. William Warner, *Albions England* (1602 edition), pp. 70, 170–77.

15. Peter Ure, in his recent edition of the play, finds it combining in Warbeck and Katherine "heroism" and "civility" while at the same time affirming, especially in Henry, the importance of able kingship. See *Perkin Warbeck* (London, 1968), lxxxii–lxxxiii.

Chapter Seven

1. Quotations from *'Tis Pity She's a Whore* come from the edition by N. W. Bawcutt for the Regents Renaissance Drama Series (Lincoln, Nebraska, 1966).
2. Oliver, *The Problem of John Ford*, p. 47.
3. See, for example, Davril, *Le Drame de John Ford*, p. 69.
4. The three most often cited are Rosset's *Histoires Tragiques* (1615), Number Five; the romance of Parthenios in Thomas Heywood's *Gunaikeion* (1624); and *Canace e Macareo* (1546) by the Italian dramatist Sperone Speroni.
5. Sidney R. Homan, Jr., finds both Shakespeare's play and *The Witch of Edmonton* formative; see "Shakespeare and Dekker as Keys to Ford's *'Tis Pity She's a Whore,*" *Studies in English Literature*, VII (Spring, 1967), 269–76. Cyrus Hoy believes Ford more indebted to Marlowe's *Doctor Faustus;* see "'Ignorance in Knowledge': Marlowe's Faustus and Ford's Giovanni," *Modern Philology*, LVII (February, 1960), 145–54.
6. Bawcutt (ed.), *'Tis Pity She's a Whore*, p. xiii.
7. Muriel C. Bradbrook, *Themes and Conventions of Elizabethan Tragedy* (Cambridge, 1935), p. 256.
8. Madeleine Doran, *Endeavors of Art* (Madison, 1954), p. 301.

Chapter Eight

1. Quotations from *Love's Sacrifice* come from the Gifford and Dyce edition.
2. Sargeaunt, *John Ford*, p. 112.
3. Davril, *Le Drame de John Ford*, pp. 171–72.
4. See Peter Ure, "Cult and Initiates in Ford's 'Love's Sacrifice,'" *Modern Language Quarterly*, XI (September, 1950), 298–306; and Herbert W. Hoskins, "A Critical Edition of *Love's Sacrifice*, by John Ford" (unpublished dissertation: Columbia, 1963), Introduction.
5. Ure, "Cult and Initiates in Ford's 'Love's Sacrifice,'" pp. 302 and 304.
6. Quotations from *The Platonic Lovers* come from the *Dramatic Works of Sir William D'Avenant*, James Maidment and W. H. Logan, eds. (London, 1872–74), I.
7. See Chapter 5, notes 5 and 6.

Chapter Nine

1. Quotations from both plays come from the Gifford and Dyce edition.
2. Ewing, *Burtonian Melancholy in the Plays of John Ford*, pp. 28–32.
3. Oliver, *The Problem of John Ford*, p. 121.

Chapter Ten

1. See *The Diary of Samuel Pepys*.
2. Edward Phillips, *Theatrum Poetarum* (London, 1675), p. 109; Wil-

liam Winstanley, *The Lives of the Most Famous English Poets* (London, 1687), p. 114; and Gerard Langbaine, *An Account of the English Dramatick Poets* (Oxford, 1691 edition), pp. 219 and 222.

3. David E. Baker, *Biographia Dramatica* (London, 1812 edition), II, 391–92, and III, 340.

4. Charles Lamb, *Specimens of English Dramatic Poets* (London, 1890 edition), p. 228.

5. *Ibid.*

6. William Hazlitt, *Lectures on the Literature of the Age of Elizabeth* (London, 1884 edition), pp. 135–43.

7. *Ibid.*, p. 142.

8. James R. Lowell, *Conversations on Some of the Old Poets* (New York, 1901 edition), pp. 225, 239–56.

9. Algernon C. Swinburne, "John Ford," *The Complete Works of Algernon Charles Swinburne*, Sir Edmund Gosse and Thomas J. Wise, eds. (London, 1926), II, 371–406.

10. *Ibid.*, II, 373, 376–77.

11. Havelock Ellis (ed.), *John Ford*, Mermaid Series (London, 1888), Introduction.

12. Hippolyte A. Taine, *Histoire de la Littérature Anglaise* (Paris, 1866 edition), II, 64 and 89.

13. George Saintsbury, *A History of Elizabethan Literature* (London, 1928 edition), pp. 403–9.

14. Felix E. Schelling, *Elizabethan Drama* (Boston, 1908), pp. 327–33; Ashley H. Thorndike, *Tragedy* (Boston, 1908), p. 229; and Stuart P. Sherman, "Forde's Contribution to the Decadence of the Drama," in *John Fordes Dramatische Werke*, W. Bang, ed. (Louvain, 1908), vii–xix.

15. T. S. Eliot, *Elizabethan Essays* (London, 1934), pp. 135–52.

16. Sargeaunt, *John Ford*, Appendix I.

17. Una Ellis-Fermor, *The Jacobean Drama* (London, 1953 edition), p. 241.

18. Ewing, *Burtonian Melancholy in the Plays of John Ford*, pp. 32–91.

19. Sensabaugh, *The Tragic Muse of John Ford*, p. 175.

20. Davril, *Le Drame de John Ford*, pp. 425–72.

21. Oliver, *The Problem of John Ford*, pp. 122–30.

22. Leech, *John Ford and the Drama of his Time*, pp. 8 and 9.

23. *Ibid.*, pp. 15 and 26.

24. Mark Stavig, *John Ford and the Traditional Moral Order* (Madison, 1968), pp. 96, 122, and 183.

Selected Bibliography

PRIMARY SOURCES

1. Seventeenth-Century Editions
A. Plays
    The Lover's Melancholy. Quarto printed in 1629.
    The Broken Heart. Q. 1633.
    'Tis Pity She's a Whore. Q. 1633.
    Love's Sacrifice. Q. 1633.
    Perkin Warbeck. Q. 1634.
    The Fancies Chaste and Noble. Q. 1638.
    The Lady's Trial. Q. 1639.
    The Queen. Q. 1653. (Probably by Ford.)
    The Spanish Gypsy. Qq. 1653, 1661. (Possibly by Ford.)
    The Sun's Darling. Qq. 1656, 1657. (With Dekker.)
    The Witch of Edmonton. Q. 1658. (With Dekker and Rowley.)
B. Nondramatic Works
    Fame's Memorial. Q. 1606. Ms. (?).
    Honour Triumphant. Q. 1606.
    Christ's Bloody Sweat. Q. 1613. (Probably by Ford.)
    The Golden Mean. 1613, 1614. (Probably by Ford.)
    A Line of Life. 1620. Ms. (?).
2. Collected Editions
    BANG, W. *John Fordes Dramatische Werke.* Louvain: A. Uystpruyst, 1908. Contains *The Lover's Melancholy* and *Love's Sacrifice;* follows exactly the quartos, including their orthography, but lists no variants.
    COLERIDGE, HARTLEY. *The Dramatic Works of Massinger and Ford.* London: Routledge, Warne, and Routledge, 1840. The Old Dramatists. With introduction and glossaries.
    DE VOCHT, H. *John Ford's Dramatic Works.* Louvain: Uystpruyst, 1927. A continuation of Bang's edition (and editorial procedure), it is composed of Ford's five other plays.
    DYCE, ALEXANDER and WILLIAM GIFFORD. *The Works of John Ford.*

3 vols. London: J. Toovey, 1869 and 1895. A revision, with additions to text and notes, of Gifford's 1827 editions. The 1895 edition was reissued by Russell & Russell, Inc., in 1965; essentially Gifford's, it remains the most widely used edition of Ford, and is the only collection that includes some of his earlier, nondramatic pieces. Introduction shows some critical insight; text usually reliable, though based upon little if any collating of various copies of seventeenth-century editions.

ELLIS, HAVELOCK. *John Ford*. London: T. Fisher Unwin, 1888. Mermaid Series. Five plays, with a short introduction stressing Ford's modernity.

GIFFORD, W. *The Dramatic Works of John Ford*. 2 vols. London: J. Murray, 1827. Revised by Dyce (see above) in 1869.

————. *The Dramatic Works of John Ford*. 2 vols. New York: J. & J. Harper, 1831. Harper's Family Library. The text and most of the explanatory notes are Gifford's; introductions to the eight plays included are by another, unidentified. Conspicuously absent is *'Tis Pity She's a Whore*.

WEBER, HENRY. *The Dramatic Works of John Ford*. 2 vols. Edinburgh: George Ramsey & Co., 1811. First modern edition of Ford; textually inferior, but some perceptive commentary.

3. Some Editions of Single Works

The Broken Heart

ANDERSON, DONALD K., JR. Lincoln: University of Nebraska Press, 1968. Regents Renaissance Drama Series.

MORRIS, BRIAN. New York: Hill and Wang, 1966. The New Mermaids.

SCOLLARD, CLINTON. New York: H. Holt and Company, 1895.

SMEATON, OLIPHANT. London: J. M. Dent and Co., 1906. The Temple Dramatists.

Perkin Warbeck

ANDERSON, DONALD K., JR. Lincoln: University of Nebraska Press, 1965. Regents Renaissance Drama Series.

PICKBURN, J. P. and J. LeGAY BRERETON. Sydney: George Robertson & Co., 1896.

STRUBLE, MILDRED C. Seattle: University of Washington Press, 1926. University of Washington Publications in Language and Literature.

URE, PETER. London: Methuen & Co. Ltd., 1968. Revels Plays.

The Queen

BANG, W. Louvain: A. Uystpruyst, 1906. *Materialen*.

'Tis Pity She's a Whore

BAWCUTT, N. W. Lincoln: University of Nebraska Press, 1966. Regents Renaissance Drama Series.

SHERMAN, S. P. Boston and London: D. C. Heath & Co., c. 1915. With *The Broken Heart* in the Belles Lettres Series.

SECONDARY SOURCES

ANDERSON, DONALD K., JR. "The Date and Handwriting of a Manuscript Copy of Ford's *Perkin Warbeck*," *Notes and Queries*, X (September, 1963), 340–41. Both internal and external evidence is cited to establish 1745 as the date of composition and to contend that several scribes, not one, were involved.

————. "The Heart and the Banquet: Imagery in Ford's *'Tis Pity* and *The Broken Heart*," *Studies in English Literature*, II (Spring, 1962), 209–17. Ford's sustained use of both heart and banquet imagery is found in both plays.

————. "Kingship in Ford's *Perkin Warbeck*," *ELH* (September, 1960), 177–93. Claims kingship an important element in the play, an idealized Henry VII being contrasted with James IV and Warbeck.

BABB, LAWRENCE. "Abnormal Psychology in John Ford's *Perkin Warbeck*," *Modern Language Notes*, LI (1936), 234–37. Finds the characterization of Warbeck influenced by Burtonian psychology.

BARISH, JONAS A. "*Perkin Warbeck* as Anti-History," *Essays in Criticism*, XX (1970), 151–71. Contends that Ford invites us to consider Warbeck as a rightful claimant to the throne.

BENTLEY, GERALD E. *The Jacobean and Caroline Stage.* Oxford: Clarendon Press, 1941–56. 5 vols. Provides important facts and well-informed opinions on the printing, licensing, and performing of Ford's plays; see particularly III, 433–64.

BLAYNEY, GLENN H. "Convention, Plot, and Structure in *The Broken Heart*," *Modern Philology*, LVI (August, 1958), 1–9. Argues for the importance of the betrothal contract, violated by Ithocles in *The Broken Heart*.

BRADBROOK, MURIEL C. *Themes and Conventions of Elizabethan Tragedy.* Cambridge: The University Press, 1935. Ford's plays, split between drama and poetry, are limited in range and decadent from "attrition."

BRERETON, J. LEGAY. "The Sources of Ford's *Perkin Warbeck*," *Anglia*, XXXIV (1911), 194–234. Halle's chronicles are seen as a direct source of *Perkin Warbeck*.

DAVRIL, ROBERT. *Le Drame de John Ford.* Paris: Librairie Marcel Didier, 1954. Scholarly, perceptive study of Ford's characterization, themes, technique, dramatic emotion, language, and versification.

ELLIS, HAVELOCK (ed.) *John Ford.* Mermaid Series. London: T. F. Unwin, 1888. Calls Ford analytical and, in many ways, modern; thinks *'Tis Pity* his greatest work.

ELLIS-FERMOR, UNA. *The Jacobean Drama*. London: Methuen & Co. Ltd., 1936. Believes Ford is Middleton's successor as analyst of emotion and that *The Broken Heart* is his greatest, most mature work. Contains a perceptive description of Ford's style.

ELIOT, T. S. *Elizabethan Essays*. London: Faber & Faber Ltd., 1934. Contends that most of Ford's plays, including *'Tis Pity*, lack "symbolic value" and "inner significance"; calls *Perkin Warbeck* his best.

EWING, S. BLAINE, JR. "Burton, Ford, and *Andromana*," *PMLA*, LIV (December, 1939), 1007–17. The melancholia in *Andromana* is based upon that in Ford's dramas.

————. *Burtonian Melancholy in the Plays of John Ford*. Princeton: Princeton University Press, 1940. Documents and analyzes Burton's influence on Ford.

HARBAGE, ALFRED. "Elizabethan-Restoration Palimpsest," *Modern Language Review*, XXXV (July, 1940), 297–304. Contends that Ford, not Henry Shirley, is author of the lost *The Spanish Duke of Lerma*.

HAZLITT, WILLIAM. *Lectures on the Literature of the Age of Elizabeth*. London: George Bell and Sons, 1884 (first published in 1820). Generally critical of Ford, charging him with "artificial elaborateness," "wire-drawn sentiment," and "playing with edged tools."

HOMAN, SIDNEY R., JR. "Shakespeare and Dekker as Keys to Ford's *'Tis Pity She's a Whore*," *Studies in English Literature*, VII (Spring, 1967), 269–76. Both *Romeo and Juliet* and *The Witch of Edmonton* are regarded as formative.

HOSKINS, HERBERT W. "A Critical Edition of *Love's Sacrifice* by John Ford." Unpublished dissertation: Columbia University, 1963. The tragic result of vow-breaking is said to be the play's theme.

HOY, CYRUS. "'Ignorance in Knowledge': Marlowe's Faustus and Ford's Giovanni," *Modern Philology*, LVII (February, 1960), 145–54. Points out that both characters have intellectual pride and misuse reason with similar tragic consequences.

JEFFREY, FRANCIS. *Contributions to the Edinburgh Review*. London: Longman, Brown, Green, and Longmans, 1844 (the essay on Ford first printed in 1811). 4 vols. Thinks the dramatist's handling of characters and incident weak, but praises Annabella's death scene.

KAUFMANN, R. J. "Ford's Tragic Perspective," *Texas Studies in Literature and Language*, I (Winter, 1960), 522–37. Some of Ford's protagonists counterfeit a heroic stature that leads to tragedy.

KING, T. J. "Staging of Plays at the Phoenix in Drury Lane, 1617–42," *Theatre Notebook*, XIX (Spring, 1965), 146–66. Informative commentary on the staging of *'Tis Pity* and *Love's Sacrifice*.

LAMB, CHARLES. *Specimens of English Dramatic Poets*. London: George Bell and Sons, 1890 (first published in 1808). Sympathetic and enthusiastic comments on Ford which influence criticism of the playwright.

LEECH, CLIFFORD. *John Ford and the Drama of His Time.* London: Chatto & Windus, 1957. Sees Ford's plays and nondramatic writings as advocating an aristocratic code of resolution in adversity.

LLOYD, BERTRAM. "An Inedited MS. of Ford's *Fames Memoriall,*" *Review of English Studies,* I (1925), 93–95. Claims that the Malone manuscript, correcting the printed editions, is the original presentation copy and presumably a holograph.

———. "The Authorship of *The Welsh Ambassador,*" *Review of English Studies,* XXI (July, 1945), 192–201. Claims the anonymous play was written by Dekker and Ford.

LOWELL, JAMES R. *Conversations on Some of the Old Poets.* New York: Thomas Y. Crowell and Co., 1901. Indicts Ford for excessive excitability and for characters who, by defying inevitable death, become sentimental.

McDONALD, CHARLES O. "The Design of John Ford's *The Broken Heart*: A Study in the Development of Caroline Sensibility," *Studies in Philology,* LIX (April, 1962), 141–61. Central to *The Broken Heart* is the notion of honor or reason controlling passion.

OLIVER, HAROLD J. *The Problem of John Ford.* Carlton, Victoria: Melbourne University Press, 1955. Finds the playwright an analyst, as well as an experimenter who sometimes anticipates techniques of modern novelists.

ORNSTEIN, ROBERT. *The Moral Vision of Jacobean Tragedy.* Madison: The University of Wisconsin Press, 1960. Ford's dramas are viewed as aristocratic rather than popular entertainment; principal conflict of *'Tis Pity* is between nature and legalistic, authoritarian religion.

RIBNER, IRVING. "By Nature's Light: The Morality of *'Tis Pity She's a Whore,*" *Tulane Studies in English,* X (1960), 39–50. The play not decadent, for it depicts the inadequacy of human and divine institutions.

———. *Jacobean Tragedy.* London: Methuen & Co. Ltd., 1962. Fordian tragedy is characterized by a skepticism often resolved in paradox.

RUSSELL, H. K. "Tudor and Stuart Dramatizations of the Doctrines of Natural and Moral Philosophy," *Studies in Philology,* XXXI (January, 1934), 1–27. Sees *The Sun's Darling* combining elements from the morality play and the masque.

SAINTSBURY, GEORGE. *A History of Elizabethan Literature.* London: Macmillan and Co., 1928. Attributes "decadence" to Ford; compares him unfavorably with Baudelaire and Flaubert.

SARGEAUNT, M. JOAN. *John Ford.* Oxford: Basil Blackwell, 1935. First book-length study of Ford; contains valuable biographical information.

SCHELLING, FELIX E. *Elizabethan Drama.* Boston and New York: Houghton

Mifflin & Co., 1908. 2 vols. In chapter entitled "Decadent Romance," finds Ford misusing his powers of analysis and casuistry, and calls *'Tis Pity* a "monstrous creation."

SENSABAUGH, GEORGE F. "John Ford Revisited," *Studies in English Literature*, IV (Spring, 1964), 196–216. Ford's belief in the discontinuity of experience accounts for his appeal to modern readers.

————. *The Tragic Muse of John Ford*. Stanford University: Stanford University Press, 1944. Argues for Ford's modernity on basis of his "scientific determinism" and "unbridled individualism."

SHERMAN, STUART P. "Forde's Contribution to the Decadence of the Drama," *John Fordes Dramatische Werke*. Ed. W. Bang. Louvain: A. Uystpruyst, 1908. Though charging Ford with decadence, also views him as creator of the problem play.

————. "Stella and *The Broken Heart*," *PMLA*, XIV (1909), 274–85. Suggests as a source for *The Broken Heart* the relationship between Sir Philip Sidney and Penelope Devereux.

STAVIG, MARK. *John Ford and the Traditional Moral Order*. Madison: University of Wisconsin Press, 1968. Contends that Ford supports, rather than challenges, the traditional moral order.

STRUBLE, MILDRED C. (ed.). *A Critical Edition of Ford's Perkin Warbeck*. Seattle: University of Washington Press, 1926. Ford viewed as challenging Stuart absolutism and the theory of divine right.

————. "The Indebtedness of Ford's 'Perkin Warbeck' to Gainsford," *Anglia*, XLIX (1926), 80–91. Gainsford's *True and Wonderful History of Perkin Warbeck* is a direct source of Ford's play.

SWINBURNE, ALGERNON C. *The Complete Works of Algernon Charles Swinburne*. Eds. Sir Edmund Gosse and Thomas J. Wise. London: William Heinemann, 1925–27. 20 vols. States that Ford, though lacking pure imagination, has great intellectual force; praises *'Tis Pity* and *The Broken Heart*.

SYKES, H. DUGDALE. *Sidelights on Elizabethan Drama*. London: Oxford University Press, 1924. Contends Ford the sole author of both *The Queen* and *The Spanish Gypsy*.

TAINE, HIPPOLYTE A. *Histoire de la Littérature Anglaise*. Paris: Hachette, 1866. 5 vols. Complimentary; sees Ford as having reached the limits of tragedy and as having written "sincere melodrama."

TANNENBAUM, SAMUEL A. *John Ford (A Concise Bibliography)*. New York: S. A. Tannenbaum, 1941. Valuable listing of primary and secondary sources, containing three hundred and eighty-five entries.

THORNDIKE, ASHLEY H. *Tragedy*. Boston and New York: Houghton Mifflin & Company, 1908. Thinks Ford decadent because of sensationalism and "mawkish" sentiment.

URE, PETER. "Cult and Initiates in Ford's 'Love's Sacrifice,'" *Modern Lan-*

guage Quarterly, XI (September, 1950), 298–306. Bianca is said to be incapable of Platonic love and to encourage Fernando to break his vow.

————. "Marriage and the Domestic Drama in Heywood and Ford," *English Studies*, XXXII (October, 1951), 200–216. Marriage as a social, domestic theme appears in both *A Woman Killed with Kindness* and *The Broken Heart*.

Index

(The works of Ford are listed under his name)

Antony, Mark, 22
Aristotle, 22, 30
Arundel, Earl of, 21
Augustine, St., 30

Bacon, Sir Francis, 15, 27, 79, 80, 81, 86
Baker, David, 134
Bancroft, Thomas, 16
Bandello, Matteo, 64
Bang, W., 42–43
Barnes, Barnabe, 64
Barnevelt, Sir John van Olden, 30, 31, 82
Bawcutt, N. W., 94
Beaumont, Francis, 50, 95–97
Beeston, Christopher, 15, 61, 77
Beeston, William, 37
Bentley, Gerald, 37, 61
Blount, Charles, 17–21
Bradbrook, Muriel, 105
Breton, Nicholas, 17
Brutus, 31
Burton, Robert, 15, 44, 45, 47, 49–50, 64, 81, 136
Byron, Duke of, 30, 31

Caesar, Julius, 22
Cervantes, Miguel de, 41
Chapman, George, 13
Charles I, 13, 37, 64, 80, 136; Caroline England, 15, 137
Charles Edward, 80

Cicero, 30
Cleopatra, 22
Clifford, Sir Robert, 78, 90
Collier, J. P., 23
Crashaw, Richard, 49
Crawford, Earl of, 90

Daliell, Lord, 78, 83, 89–90, 140
Daniel, Samuel, 17
D'Avenant, Sir William, 113–14
Davies, Sir John, 17
Davril, Robert, 26, 44–45, 64, 107, 135–36
Dawbney, Lord, 79
Dekker, Thomas, 13, 33, 35, 36, 37–38, 40, 140
Devereux, Penelope, 18, 22, 64; see also Lady Rich
Devonshire, Earl of, see Charles Blount
Doncaster, Viscount, 26
Doran, Madeleine, 105
Dunkel, W. D., 41
Durham, Bishop of, 78, 88, 90–91

Edward IV, 77, 84
Eliot, T. S., 133, 135
Elizabeth I, Queen, 13, 18–19, 107; Elizabethan, 43, 74, 102, 137, 141
Ellis, Havelock, 134–35
Ellis-Fermor, Una, 41, 135–36
Epaminondas of Thebes, 31
Essex, Earl of, 18–19, 27, 30, 31
Ewing, S. Blaine, Jr., 43–44, 64, 136

Ferdinand, Emperor, 78
Fletcher, John, 13, 14, 15, 23, 50, 73–74, 95–97, 121, 137; Fletcherian, 119
Fletcher, Joseph, 26
Ford, Henry (brother), 16
Ford, John (great-grandfather), 16
Ford, John:

WORKS:

Bristowe Merchant, The, 33
Broken Heart, The, 13, 14, 15, 18, 19, 21, 24, 25, 26, 27, 36–37, 39, 43, 44, 46, 47, 49, 61–76, 77, 81–83, 89, 93, 97, 99, 105, 106, 107, 117, 118, 134, 135, 137–38, 139, 140, 141
Christ's Bloody Sweat, 17, 23–26, 30, 32, 37, 136
Fairy Knight, The, 33
Fame's Memorial, 16, 17–21, 24, 25–26, 29, 30, 32, 64
Fancies, Chaste and Noble, The, 43, 49, 119–26, 132, 137, 139
Golden Mean, The, 17, 26–29, 30, 32, 81–82, 136, 142
Honour Triumphant or the Peeres Challenge, 16, 17, 21–23, 24, 32, 64, 66, 142
Lady's Trial, The, 16, 24, 37, 46, 74, 99, 119, 126–32, 133–34, 139–40, 141
Late Murther of the Son upon the Mother, A, 33
Line of Life, A, 17, 26, 29–32, 80, 82
Lover's Melancholy, The, 15, 33, 39–40, 43, 44, 45, 46, 47–60, 61, 66–67, 77, 81, 82–83, 90, 92, 105, 106, 107, 117–18, 134, 137, 138, 139
Love's Sacrifice, 14, 15, 39–40, 44, 46, 92, 99, 102, 107–18, 119, 128, 137, 138, 139–40, 141–42
Monarches Meeting, The, 21
Perkin Warbeck (The Chronicle History of), 14, 15, 19, 20, 21, 27, 32, 36–37, 39–40, 43, 44, 46, 67, 77–91, 97, 105, 106, 107, 117, 134, 137, 138–39, 140, 142
Queen, or the Excellency of her Sex, The, 34, 40–41, 42–46, 50, 135, 137, 138, 139–40
Sir Thomas Overbury's Ghost, 17
Spanish Gypsy, The, 34, 40–42, 46
Sun's Darling, The, 33–34, 37–40, 43, 46
'Tis Pity She's a Whore, 13, 14, 15, 22, 23–24, 39–40, 47, 92–106, 107, 117, 119, 133, 134–35, 137–38, 139, 141–42
Witch of Edmonton, The, 33–37, 38, 40, 41, 46
Ford, Thomas (father), 16
Frederick, Elector Palatine, 80
Frion, Stephen, 84, 88

Gainsford, Thomas, 79, 81, 85–86, 89
Gifford, William, 64
Goodcole, Henry, 34
Gordon, Lady Katherine, 77, 78–79, 80, 84, 89–90, 91, 138–39, 140, 142
Grosart, A. B., 23

Hall, Edward, 86
Hannibal, 29, 31
Harbage, Alfred, 33
Harrington, Lord John, 30, 31
Hazlitt, William, 64, 133–34
Heminge, William, 16
Henrietta Maria, Queen, 64, 113, 136
Henry VII, 20, 29, 32, 77–80, 82–83, 84, 85–89, 90–91, 105, 139
Herbert, Sir Henry, 16
Heywood, Thomas, 16, 107
Hialas, (de Ayala), Don Pedro, 78, 88, 90
Holinshed, Raphael, 86
Horace, 30
Hunter, Joseph, 23
Huntley, Earl of, 78, 83–84, 87, 89–90, 139

Jacobean, 137
James I, 19, 20, 30, 32
James IV of Scotland, 40, 77–78, 79–91, 105, 140
Jonson, Ben, 13, 14, 121

Kyd, Thomas, 21, 140

La Cerda, Mexia de, 64
Lamb, Charles, 133–34
Langbaine, Gerald, 134
Laud, William, 18
Lawrence, W. W., 37
Leech, Clifford, 23, 136–37
Lennox, Duke of, 21
Lloyd, Bertram, 18
Lowell, James Russell, 133–34, 142

Machiavelli, 86
Machin, Lewis, 44
Margaret of Burgundy, 77
Margaret, Princess of England, 78, 80
Markham, Gervase, 44
Marlowe, Christopher, 13, 14
Marston, John, 15, 64
Massinger, Philip, 13, 80, 137
Middleton, Thomas, 13, 34, 40–41, 46, 105, 135, 140
Montgomery, Countess of, 21
Moseley, Humphrey, 33
Mountjoy, Lord James, 18
Mountjoy, Lord, see Charles Blount
Mowbray, Thomas, 29

Nashe, Thomas, 24
Neoplatonic, 139; Neoplatonism, 113, 136
Nero, 31
Norfolk, Duke of, 233 Thomas Mowbray
Northumberland, Earl of, 26, 27

Oliver, Harold, 24, 26, 30, 36, 38, 41, 92, 119, 136
O'Neill, Hugh, 19
Ovid, 29

Parliament, 137
Pausanias, 64
Pembroke, Countess of, 21, 24; Earl of, 21, 23
Pepys, Samuel, 133–34
Peterborough, Earl of, 92
Philips, Ambrose, 49
Phillips, Edward, 134
Phocion of Athens, 31
Phormio, 31
Plantagenet, 87
Plato, 40
Platonic, 64–66, 73, 113–16, 118; Platonism, 15, 23, 39
Pliny, 30
Plutarch, 30
Pompey, 27, 29
Ptolemy, 27

Raleigh, Sir Walter, 30, 31
Restoration, 133
Rich, Lady Penelope, 17, 18, 22
Rich, Lord, 18, 64
Richard, Duke of York, 77–78, 81
Richard II, 29
Richard III, 29, 79
Rowley, William, 33–34, 35, 36, 40–41, 46
Russell, H. K., 38

Saintsbury, George, 134–35
Sargeaunt, Joan, 23–24, 26, 38, 41–42, 117, 135
Schelling, Felix, 135
Scipio Africanus, 29
Sejanus, 27
Seneca, 31
Sensabaugh, George, 64, 136–37
Shakespeare, William, 13, 14, 15, 61, 79, 84, 93, 138; *Antony and Cleopatra*, 135; *King Lear*, 49–50; *Othello*, 15, 107, 110–11, 128, 142; *Richard II*, 15, 79; *Romeo and Juliet*, 15, 93, 102, 135; *Titus Andronicus*, 140, 142
Sherman, Stuart, 18, 42, 135
Shirley, James, 13, 119, 137

Sidney, Sir Philip, 18, 64, 107
Simnel, Lambert, 78, 84, 91, 139
Socrates, 30
Stanley, Sir William, 78, 86, 90
Stavig, Mark, 136–37
Stoic, 85, 97; Stoical, 14; Stoicism,
  14, 15, 19, 27, 30, 32, 44, 46, 68,
  71, 77, 82, 84, 91
Strada, Famianus, 49, 51
Stuart absolutism, 79; dramatists,
  74; dynasty, 80, 84; period, 102;
  Pretender, 80
Surrey, Earl of, 88–89, 91
Sykes, H. Dugdale, 36, 38, 41–42
Sylvester, Joshua, 17
Swinburne, Algernon Charles, 133–
  35

Taine, Hippolyte, 134–35
Thorndike, Ashley, 135
Tourneur, Cyril, 140
Tudor dynasty, 80, 84
Tyrone, Earl of, see Hugh O'Neill

Urswick, Christopher, 81

Warbeck, Perkin, 20, 32, 36, 40,
  44, 46, 77–91, 97, 105, 139, 140,
  142
Warner, William, 89
Weber, Henry, 134
Webster, John, 13, 33, 138, 140
Wilkins, George, 64
Winstanley, William, 134
Wolsey, Cardinal, 27